AMERICANA

1925

Terence Shone

march 1926.

AMERICANA

1925

EDITED BY

H. L. MENCKEN

Editor of THE AMERICAN MERCURY

LONDON : MARTIN HOPKINSON & CO.
LTD., 14 HENRIETTA STREET, COVENT
GARDEN, W.C.2   1925

PRINTED IN GREAT BRITAIN.
CHISWICK PRESS : CHARLES WHITTINGHAM AND GRIGGS (PRINTERS), LTD.
TOOKS COURT, CHANCERY LANE, LONDON.

PREFACE

This collection is the work of hundreds of readers of THE AMERICAN MERCURY—so many, indeed, that it would be impracticable to acknowledge individually the editor's debts to them. With a few exceptions, every collector has confined himself to his own State. In consequence the selections show a variety that no single collector could have hoped to match. They come in part from newspapers of wide circulation and from other easily accessible sources, but they come in larger part from little country papers, from broadsides and other such documents of purely local circulation, and from handbills and other advertisements observed along the streets. They thus offer a singularly intimate and revelatory insight into the daily life and thought of the American people. No sociological inquiry, however elaborately planned, could get as near to the folk. Here are the things that Americans of the vast majority read every day. Here are the ideas that are regularly presented to them. Here are impromptu, unposed portraits of the prophets and sorcerers who lead them.

Superficially, the collection may seem to belong to humor. As printed from month to month in THE AMERICAN MERCURY it has unquestionably caused some cackles. Contributions to it from connoisseurs of the preposterous pour in by the thousand. There are multitudes of protests

PREFACE

whenever the rumor spreads—it has been spread at intervals by enemies to the magazine, some of them in high political and ecclesiastical office—that the department is to be suppressed by the *Polizei*, or otherwise abandoned. But those who see only humor in these fantastic paragraphs see only half that is in them. Fundamentally, nine tenths of them are serious in intent, and they are all presented here for a quite serious purpose. That purpose, one of the main aims of THE AMERICAN MERCURY, is to make the enlightened minority of Americans familiar, by documentary evidence, with what is going on in the minds of the masses—the great herd of undifferentiated good-humored, goose-stepping, superstitious, sentimental, credulous, striving, romantic American people. Some of the ideas cherished by that herd are obviously insane. Many others stand in sharp opposition to everything that civilized men regard as decorous and for the common weal. But it must be obvious that no headway can be made in opposing and changing those ideas until it is known clearly what they are. The following collection is presented as material to that end. It may not be completely comprehensive, but certainly no man of enough first-hand knowledge to speak at all will deny that it is thoroughly and representatively American. It strikes notes that are as unmistakably American as the sound of a jazz band, a revival hymn or a college yell. It drips with the juices of Kiwanis, the American Legion, the Ku Klux, Rotary, the Mystic Shrine, the Elks, the Sons of the Revolution and the Y.M.C.A. It is genuine home-brew.

If the present collection wins any esteem among scholars it will be followed by others at intervals of a year or two.

PREFACE

The material is in constant flux. The changes in it are interesting and important. Not only do the transient crazes of the populace change from year to year; their fundamental ideas also change. In 1915 the Ku Klux Klan was unheard of; in 1925 it is one of the most powerful factors in American life, politically, socially and theologically. The radio is vastly transforming the notions of both the peasantry and the city proletariat, as the moving-picture did before it, and the telephone before the moving-picture. The low-caste American is perhaps the most ardent of hero-worshippers ever heard of in the world, and his successive heroes exert a powerful influence upon his ideas and ideals. If Dr. Harding had lived the whole country would have borrowed something of his careless ease of manner; under Dr. Coolidge it is taking on a Puritan dourness. Under Wilson it wallowed in sonorous platitudes; under Roosevelt it was bellicose and sporting. Thus the evidence of what is going on behind the popular glabella must be revised periodically. This collection pretends only to deal with 1925.

Inasmuch as it is printed simultaneously in England, a glossary for English readers has been appended, together with certain other notes for their information.

October 1, 1925.

H. L. MENCKEN.

CONTENTS

ix   b

CONTENTS

AMERICANA

1925

ALABAMA

I

Sententious ethical note from the Alabama *Christian Advocate*:

> May a Christian dance? Of course, he may. He may swear and lie too, but it wouldn't make him a better Christian. Surely, Christian, you may dance, but dancing will never identify you as a Christian. What puzzles me is that you ask the question so often. Christians who don't dance never ask it. Yes, Christian, dance if you can't live without it. Join hands with Salome, Herodias and Herod, and circle to the left; but don't be surprised if you are mistaken for a goat.

2

Literary criticism in Birmingham, from the distinguished *News*:

> Richard Le Gallienne does not specify. He does not drag the shrinking literary violets from their tiny niches and push them out on the stage and say this one will save you from despair, this from the social smut of your Sherwood Lawrences and your Rupert Hughes, this from the bitter cynicism of your modern imitators of Nietzsche and others who declare the earth is a Sorrowful Star and something to be endured in a sort of dreary ennui. But it is a comforting thought to remember that for every Robert Keable fashioning abnormalities there's

I   B an Edward C. Venable dreaming wholesome dreams—for every sex-drenched horror like Dreiser's " Genius," there's a Christopher Morley pointing " Where the Blue Begins."

3

From a bull, *De cigaretto*, issued by a distinguished spiritual leader of Birmingham:

Cigarettes kill character. . . . The fight for the next ten years is to save the generation from cigarettes.

4

The perils of amour among the white, Protestant Nordics along the Coosa river, as described in a Gadsden dispatch:

Smith Hill is in the county jail on the charge of assault to murder. It is claimed that he was passing the home of his rival, Sam Aiken, in East Gadsden, when he saw him standing in front of a mirror arranging his necktie. Hill decided to put him out of business, it is charged, and so pulled a revolver and fired. The bullet passed close by Aiken's head and shattered the mirror.

5

The intellectual life in Montgomery, as reported by the eminent *Journal*:

The meeting of the Pilot Club was held in the Philathea room of the Court Street Methodist Church. . . . A unique feature of the meeting was an oration on Woodrow Wilson by little Vaughn Robison, son of Mr. and Mrs. E. V. Robison. He also gave " The Alabaman's Creed," by Judge Walter B. Jones. Miss

Lucy Dowe made an interesting talk on " Coca-Cola." Miss Dowe also donated a case of coca-cola, which was won by Miss Ellen Jackson.

6

Difficulties of a poor man in the faubourgs of Birmingham, as described in an open letter to the celebrated Birmingham *News*:

To the Editor The Birmingham *News*:

I am a resident of Ensley, having been in this place for the past twenty years. I am a taxpayer, a voter and also a property-owner. One-armed man, pure white, work at steel plant for an honest living, and in good standing. I feel as if I have been treated unjustly. My cow strayed from my yard this morning and I immediately went to the pound pen and notified the head man in charge that my cow had got out and to 'phone me as soon as he had heard or seen her. A few hours previous to this conversation I sent my boy to the pound pen to see if my cow was there, and she was. They had milked her and got about four gallons of milk, and charged me $2.50 to get her out. Now, this cow had only been caught about two hours and the poundkeeper never reported to me he had ever seen or heard of her. He said it was his duty to milk all cows. Now I want to say, if the City of Birmingham is in such hard circumstances that when they catch a man's cow and have to milk her and then charge him $2.50 in addition to get her out, they had better call a referendum for another bond issue and beg the people to support it.

J. W. CAWTHORNE.

1723 Avenue H, Ensley.

3

7

Incidents of the Christian life in the back country:

Robertsdale Klan, No. 78, appeared at the Baptist Church at Summerdale last night and presented Rev. Kimbrough with a beautiful new Bible to replace the one destroyed several weeks ago by vandals who entered the church at night, tore up the Bible and then locked goats in the building.

8

Field sports in the same region, from the archives of the Committee on the Judiciary of the House of Representatives:

Helena, Ala.: After protecting himself against a mob for six hours John King, employed in the mines, was lynched by men whom he had accused of taking money from his pay-envelope.

Adamsville, Ala.: Will McBride, 60 years old, was taken from bed by a mob and beaten to death. He had been arrested on a charge of assault but dismissed by the judge. Some school children had become frightened at seeing him walk along the road.

9

Final triumph of Calvinism in Birmingham:

Birmingham's exclusive clubs—and all other kinds—will be as blue hereafter as city and State laws can make them. Commissioner of Safety W. C. Bloe issued an order today that Sunday golf, billiards and *dominoes* be stopped, beginning tomorrow.

ARIZONA

I

Progress of Christian enlightenment in the land of the
barbarous Hopis and Zuñis, as revealed by a sermon by
the Rev. Dr. John B. Andrews, of University Methodist
Church, Tucson:

> I believe that the whale swallowed Jonah.

2

Sweet, lovely and well-deserved words from the eminent
Tucson *Citizen*:

> There is nothing so responsive as an Elk's heart. In
> the social sense, he is the courtier, the gallant knight of
> modern times. There is more Christianity in the day-
> by-day practices of Elkdom than there is in many a
> monumental cathedral. There has been nothing
> spiritually finer since the day of the Christian crusaders
> than the Elks' financing the relief work of the Salvation
> Army during the World War.

3

Sinister dispatch from the rising town of Winslow in the
El Paso *Fiery Cross*:

> On their way back to the Klavern the Klansmen en-
> countered a typical representative of that miserable and

5

undesirable class of individuals so long recognized as a menace to America and its institutions. He was easily recognized as a foreigner by the blank look of ignorance upon his face and the bold effrontery with which he leered into the faces of the passing Klansmen. The fiendish glare in his eyes seemed to reflect, upon his otherwise expressionless countenance, the murderous thoughts in his soul. But he was alone and his kind, as a rule, work only in mobs, for they are cowards at heart.

4

Fate of the First Amendment to the Constitution in the sage brush country, as reported by a Nogales dispatch to the Tucson *Daily Star:*

George L. Patrick, of Seattle, Wash., a civil engineer, will probably spend the next 200 days in the Santa Cruz county jail, as a result of getting all het up at the international line, and proceeding to say unkind words about President Coolidge. Patrick arrived here several days ago with the intention of crossing the border with two burros on a prospecting trip down the west coast of Mexico. He tried to get a permit from the Customs Service to take a rifle across the line and when shown a telegram from President Coolidge stating that an embargo had been placed on firearms and advised that he would have to get a permit from Washington, he is alleged to have replied: " To h——— with Coolidge; it's only an accident that he is President." A complaint was filed against the man and Justice of the Peace Charles Hardy gave him his choice of paying a $200 fine or serving 200 days in jail. He chose the latter.

5

Extension of bibliomania to the great open spaces, where red-blooded he-men still roam the primeval lava, as reported by the Tucson *Star:*

> Harold Bell Wright is personally autographing every copy of " The Mine With the Iron Door " that is sold by the Wyatt book store. Mr. Wright also has had an extra page inserted in these books containing a picture of himself and the entrance gate leading into the patio of his home.

6

From an harangue delivered to the Chamber of Commerce of Tucson by the Hon. H. B. Titcomb:

> The person who objects to the ringing of cracked bells from a church-tower I do not believe is a good citizen of any community.

7

What happens when the vices of Babylon penetrate to the wilds, as disclosed by a Winkelman dispatch:

> Over-devotion to the radio is said to have been a contributing cause for the suicide of Russell Baker, who tied a heavy iron bar to his neck and then jumped into a deep pool. He is said to have become a nervous wreck through loss of sleep. At his work he talked incessantly of the radio and apparently forgot his wife and three children.

8

Rules posted in the bed chambers of the McNeil Hotel, the principal hostelry of the rising town of Miami:

McNEIL HOTEL RULES

MIAMI, ARIZONA

No man, men or male persons are allowed in a room, which is occupied by a lady or ladies or female person or persons.

No lady, ladies or female person or persons are allowed in a room which is occupied by a man, men or male person or persons, unless they are registered as man and wife.

No man, men or male person or persons, or no lady, ladies or female person or persons shall occupy a room or a bed with another person, without first consulting the management of the hotel and registering on the date of beginning of occupancy of the room.

I will call your attention to Chapter 62, House Bill No. 4, against lewdness, assignation, prostitution or nuisance which was voted on the fifteenth day of November, 1918, and the same became a State law.

J. P. McNEIL, *Proprietor.*

ARKANSAS

1

Rise of the tone art in the swamps along the Arkansas river, as shown by the programme of a concert by the Carr Quartette at Little Rock:

QUARTETTE: " Some Folks Say a Nigger Won't Steal."
BASS SOLO: " The Life of a Married Man."
QUARTETTE: " Don't Be a Monkey Man."
TENOR SOLO: " Hush, Someone is Calling My Name! "

2

Progress of reform in Little Rock, as reported by the estimable Arkansas *Democrat:*

Warden Evans announced that all electrocutions conducted under his regime would be held strictly according to the law as regards witnesses. " People get the idea," he said, " that electrocutions are social gatherings, but none of this kind will be held while I am warden. *An execution is a serious matter* and should be considered as such."

3

The Higher Learning at the University of Arkansas, as described in a dispatch from Fayetteville:

Joseph, the lad who wore the coat of fifty-seven varieties of colors, was the world's first life insurance

9

agent, declared L. A. Boli of Wichita, Kansas, vice-president of the National Savings Life Insurance Company, in an address before the insurance class of the University of Arkansas. Joseph, he added, provided during the seven years of plenty for the following seven lean years. The writing of life insurance, the speaker declared, is next in importance to the preaching of the gospel.

4

Dispatch from the up and coming Arkansas town of Stuttgart in the Little Rock *Gazette:*

The Rev. Dr. M. M. Culpepper, pastor of the Grand Avenue Methodist Church, in discussing National Music Week at the request of the local Musical Club, scored the members for devoting their time to the study of grand opera, which, he said, " no one can understand, and if they did, it would do them no good."

5

Society note from the instructive Little Rock *Daily News:*

Much improvement was shown in the condition of Diamond Joe Sullivan today, according to a physician's report, and his complete recovery is believed assured. When attendants report him completely out of danger, Governor McRae is expected to fix the day of his execution.

6

Dispatch from Meadows Park to the eminent Newton County *Times:*

The stork flew to the home of Mr. and Mrs. P. T.

Tony on Tuesday and left a 14-pound baby boy. He was christened Davis Coolidge LaFollette Johns Farris Wallace Nations Tony.

7

Professor A. M. Harding, director of the General Extension Division at the University of Arkansas, on the public value of the radio broadcasting station maintained at the University by the learned brethren of the natural philosophy faculty:

> I do not believe all the members of our faculties appreciate the value of this broadcasting station to the University. The very fact that a man in some town in Arkansas is listening to one of our University professors is worth a great deal to the University, even if the man does not understand what the professor is talking about.

8

Didactic stanza by Obediah Harold Martin, a favorite poet of Little Rock:

> Presentable clothes make considerable effect,
> But a poor man's partaking of the foolish habit
> Of unnecessary dressing shows a considerable defect.
> Why should I dress beyond my means,
> Trying to keep up with the richest men in New Orleans,
> When I know their income is so much more than mine?
> Keeping up with them will keep me in debt all the time.
> Of course, everybody likes nice clothes to wear,
> But to go beyond your means
> You can't treat yourself nor creditors fair.

11

9

The spread of morality in the back country, as revealed by a recent addition to the statutes of the rising town of Norphelt:

ORDINANCE NO. 20

Section 1.—Hereafter, it shall be unlawful for any man and woman, male or female, to be guilty of committing the act of sexual intercourse between themselves at any place within the corporate limits of said town. . . .

Section 3.—Section One of this ordinance shall not apply to married persons, as between themselves, and their husband and wife, unless of a grossly improper and lascivious nature.

10

Announcement of a favorite physician of Cleveland county, as reported by the *Journal of the American Medical Association*:

NOTICE

To the Public:

The reason I have hitherto been able to practice medicine so much cheaper than the other doctors did was because I am a widower and have no children to support.

It's now my duty to inform the public that this advantage will shortly be withdrawn. You will therefore do well to send in your choice cases at once for the old rate.

Office at Prof. Tisdale's home, East Fourth street, Rison, Ark.

Fraternally,
DR. J. L. COOPER.

CALIFORNIA

I

Renaissance of a neglected art in the home of the movie, as reported by the Los Angeles *Times*:

In response to thousands of requests from the almost countless admirers of this famous American star, I take pride in announcing Mr. Guy Bates Post's return to the speaking stage. The consensus of many of America's foremost critics is—" His intensity disturbs and arrests. As the greatness of his genius governs the trend of thought, aroused in the genius that is—to a greater or lesser degree—the thing that governs—controls—dwarfs or magnifies—the actions—attitudes—good or bad qualities—that makes or unmakes man. By his genius compelling every auditor to feel they are parcel and part of the play—causing their pulses to throb with his, their hearts yearn—glow—ache and are glad with the beats of his heart, until actor and audience become welded as one—fused in the finesse of a single thought."

THE PLAY—" The Climax," a play filled with suspense that comes spontaneously from that soul, secreted in every normal person's breast of thinking age —interspersed with natural effervescing comedy that bubbles into chuckles and bursts into roars, causing tears to recede into the ducts from whence they came, at the critical moment when more sorrow would be anguish—more selfishness produce pain.

MELVILLE B. RAYMOND,
Director of Tour.

13

2

The awakening of conscience in Los Angeles, as reported
by the same great paper:

" To try in every legitimate way to get back to the
homely virtues and ideals of our forefathers," is the
announced purpose of the newly organized Loyal
Defenders of Pure American Girlhood, articles of
incorporation for which were filed yeſterday with the
Secretary of State at Sacramento. Los Angeles will
be the principal place of business of the corporation.

3

Mature conclusion of Miss Barbara La Marr, eminent
screen ſtar, as set forth in the inspiring *Movie Weekly:*

I think that Elbert Hubbard is the greateſt philo-
sopher that ever lived.

4

Ethical effeċts of excessive theological passion in the
capital of the New Thought and the movies:

The business men's Bible class of Long Beach, which
yeſterday reported an attendance of 31,034 in the final
session of its attendance conteſt with a similar organization of Kansas City, today was accused flatly of cheating
by J. W. Lingenfelter, representative of the Kansas City
organization.

He asserted he checked yeſterday's attendance at
Long Beach with the aid of a score of private deteċtives
armed with counting machines and that the aċtual
attendance in the Municipal Park where the gathering

was held was 13,930, or 17,104 less than the total announced.

5

Official view, in San Francisco, of the aims and usufructs of the late war, as stated in a sermon by the Rev. James L. Gordon, pastor of the First Congregational Church:

> The great war was humanity's battle for humanity. That human liberty might be preserved! That universal freedom might be perpetuated! That democracy of the world might be safeguarded! That Christianity might survive! That the world's last and best civilization should not break down!

6

Counter measures against the carnival of sin at Hollywood, as reported by the Hon. W. R. Hearst's great Christian paper, the Los Angeles *Examiner*:

> Los Angeles has been a center of continuous prayer every moment for the past twenty-two months. Since the dedication of Angelus Temple nearly two years ago, from the dark hours of midnight, through the dawn, on to midday and round the clock again there has been a steady outpouring of prayer to God that has brought down showers of blessing upon thousands and thousands of persons. Up in the Watch Tower of the temple, night or day, prayer never ceases. It is a sacred enclosure, a quiet, peaceful room, where the workers, women in the day time and men at night, in two-hour periods, pray for the spiritual illumination of the people of all nations.

15

7

Obiter dictum of Hahn, J., a favorite jurist of Los Angeles, in the case of the State vs. Brown, Guthro *et al*:

There is a line of demarcation between the spooning of persons not in love and the brand of affection displayed by young persons who have plighted their troth to each other. The first class of kisses more often precede a more serious offense, and therefore are a menace to the morals of society. The kiss of love has long been recognized by society as being on a legitimate and moral basis.

8

Treasonable but plausible remarks of a citizen of Los Angeles in *Bob Shuler's Magazine*, a favorite local publication:

Los Angeles is world-famous for three things: First, as a city where more suckers are strung and more wallets are extracted than in any other city of like size in America. Second, as a city where the marriage relation is made ridiculous and where sex-stimulation is at the maximum. Third, as a city where there are more religious vagaries, more cults and isms, more psychic manifestations and delusions, more commercialized miracles and more flagrant deceptions in the name of the gentle child, Jesus, than in any other city possibly in the entire world. Los Angeles is fertile soil for every kind of impostor that the face of the earth has been cursed by. The suckers all come here sooner or later and the whole twelve months is open season.

9

Another reason for ſtaying away from Los Angeles, as set forth in an open letter to the eminent *Daily News* of that city:

Why can't we have truthful weather reports? To read in the papers that the temperature was not below 44 degrees when we had ice frozen more than a quarter of an inch thick in our yards day after day is absurd. The point of freezing muſt have changed since I learned it. Where do they hang the official thermometer, over a furnace?

H. B. WHEELER.

10

Yet another:

Downtown cafés, hotels, clubs and other gathering places will be frequented by special inveſtigators in the rôles of waiters, check girls, entertainers, doormen, waitresses and gueſts. Policemen patrolling the ſtreets will be on the lookout for . . . confetti throwers. The anti-cigarette legion will aid in preventing women smoking. The police will censor signs on automobiles.

11

Progress of the Higher Learning at Stanford University, as reported by a press dispatch from Palo Alto:

Yell leading has been made a subjeſt in the curriculum at Stanford and credit will be given to sophomores trying out for assiſtant yell leader who regiſter in the new course. " Bleacher psychology," " the correſt use of the voice," " development of ſtage presence " and " what a coach expeſts of the yell leader " will be topics of leſtures by members of the faculty and by Prof. Andrew Kerr, football coach.

12

Want ad in Mr. Hearst's great Christian periodical, the Los Angeles *Examiner*:

WANTED: good looking stenographer; stenographic ability not essential. Apply 905 American Bank B'ldg.

13

Climax of the career of a learned American *Junker*, as described by the favorite Hollywood *News*:

A member of one of the oldest American families, Mr. Train, through his mother's family, is a second cousin of the late William Kissam Vanderbilt, and is a cousin of the present Marquis of Blandford and also of the former Duchess of Marlborough, who was Consuelo Vanderbilt. Mr. Train is a nephew of the late Admiral Charles R. Train, U.S.N., and grandson of a former attorney-general of Massachusetts. Graduating from Harvard College in 1922, Mr. Train took a postgraduate course at Magdalen College, Oxford, which was followed by extensive traveling of several months' duration on the Continent. . . . Mr. Train has joined the scenario staff of the Famous Players-Lasky Company.

14

Effects of the Volstead Act in the faubourgs of San Francisco, as reported by the *Examiner*:

Scores of young girls and youths were found stupefied by liquor in San Mateo county roadhouses by Federal Prohibition agents yesterday. Some of the girls were only 14 or 15, the agents said, while in many cases their male companions were years older. Helpless under the influence of liquor, the girls were unable to resist the attentions of the men.

15

Harsh and searching trial of the 100 per cent Americans of Berkeley, seat of the University of California, of the Snell Seminary for Girls and of the California School of Arts and Crafts, as reported by a recent press dispatch:

To test the virility of war-time patriotism, the Berkeley Post of the American Legion recently adopted a unique plan. A crisp new one-dollar greenback was sent to twenty-five citizens, erstwhile speakers in support of the Liberty Loan drives, with instructions that they were to keep the dollars providing they needed the money more than the ex-service man. But in case, as patriots, they still believed, as they professed to believe during the war, that " nothing is too good for the boys," they were to add another dollar to the one received and return both dollars to the American Legion memorial fund. Eleven kept the dollars.

16

From a list of acts forbidden by city ordinances in Los Angeles, prepared for the use of visitors:

Shooting rabbits from street cars.
Throwing snuff, or giving it to a child under sixteen.
Bathing two babies in a single bathtub at one time.
Making pickles in any downtown district.
Selling snakes on the streets.

17

Contribution to "The Power of Prayer" department of the Los Angeles *Examiner:*

An enraged cow attacked me once when I was teaching school in a rural community near Cedarville in the northern part of this State. A dairy cow was charging down the road after me, and as she drew near I realized that I was in the path of an unfuriated beast and only God could save me. I breathed an intense prayer for deliverance and instantly an inner voice guided me. I grasped her long pointed horns and held on with all my might. The beast turned into a field and began to circle round and round. I lost consciousness and when I came to she was standing still with her head to the ground. Every time she struggled a wave of strength flowed through me and I held her till help came. I now know why the lions could not touch Daniel, for Jesus is the same yesterday, today and forever.

18

From the case book of the Pisgah Home, 6044 Echo Street, Los Angeles:

CASE I.—When Sister Grace Segar came to us at Pisgah, she was in a most hopeless condition. Her pastor and friends brought her to us that she might have a Christian place in which to die. The Lord healed her and the following day she went out in the garden and hoed onions. Ten days later, she went home to assist her husband in keeping a store and bakery. They are now missionaries to the Indians in Tolchoco, Arizona.

CASE II.—Sister Smith just took some little handkerchiefs and tore them up in strips, and put them around

20

the legs of her little chickens, twenty or thirty of them that were sick, and dressed them up with little strips of cloth, and the next morning every chicken was well.

CASE III.—I want to tell about how wonderfully a cow was healed in answer to prayer. She was heavy with calf and had fallen into a ditch and laid there two days before we found her. After this, she wandered off down the creek and was there five days and nights. When found, we pulled her out with a wire cable, and as she was unable to stand, had to swing her up. While she was hanging there supported by the tackle, Brother Cheek came along and laid hands on her and asked God to heal her. The next morning she was gone, tackle and all, and when I found her, she turned and chased me up a tree.

19

Dispatch from the rising town of Danville to the San Francisco *Chronicle:*

Distribution of the communal Saturday night bath throughout the week is the solution offered for the present water shortage here by the Danville Water Company. On Saturday nights some of the residents can get no water at all. It is suggested that the inhabitants be divided alphabetically into seven groups, one section to bathe each night of the week, eliminating the drain on the water system Saturday nights.

COLORADO

Laudable development of politeness among Colorado job-holders, as reported by the *Rocky Mountain News*:

Wayne C. Williams, a young Denver attorney, was sworn in yesterday as Attorney General of Colorado to succeed the late Russell W. Fleming. After the ceremony the new Attorney General requested each person present to pause a moment in silent prayer for his predecessor.

2

How the lawmakers of this great State are inspired in their deliberations, as set forth in a current press dispatch:

To strains of music that might have emanated from a midnight cabaret, the members of the lower house of the State Assembly went through their first night session. When the solons entered the chamber an orchestra was grinding out lively tunes. Popular airs continued until adjournment at midnight. The moaning of a saxophone and the singing of several members of a chorus of a musical revue apparently mingled well with the serious business of legislating, the members continuing the introduction of scores of bills without interruption.

3

New form of divine worship among the Methodists of Steamboat Springs, as reported by the estimable *Sentinel* of that fair city:

Next Sunday an attempt will be made to read the New Testament through in one day, starting at 6 o'clock in the morning and finishing at 11.30 in the evening. Sixty-eight people will be required to do this. There will be no preaching, singing or music. The Bible will be read aloud continuously. People may come at any time and leave at any time without interrupting the reading. You may leave your offering as usual. The Marathon will be held at the Methodist church. The Rev. Maurice Habgood will start the reading.

4

Exercise in transcendental logic by a favorite Trinidad divine, as reported by the eminent *Picketwire:*

Mortal man never wrote the Bible. A good man could not have written the Bible, and a bad man would not have written it if he could. A good man could not have written it because the Bible tells us 2008 times that God Himself is the author; therefore, if man wrote the Bible, he is a great liar, and, therefore, was not a good man. And a bad man would not have written the Bible if he could, because it tells him what he is, and that is the thing he isn't wanting to believe, because if he did he could not sleep nights as long as he remained unsaved and unrepentant.

5

Working of the Holy Spirit as described by Captain S.
V. Broas, of the Salvation Army, in the Loveland *Reporter-
Herald*:

Charlie was a young man of wonderful possibilities,
but he was different from most men. God seemed to
have designated him to be a preacher or Salvation Army
Officer, for he could not get these things out of his mind,
but

HE FOUGHT AGAINST THE CALL.

I met him first at L——, my second appointment,
and he came to the mercy seat for salvation. Soon afterwards, however, he went to Chicago, whether to get a
job or to get away from God's call, I can't tell.

A year later, by special ruling of God's providence, I
was sent back to L——. God had a hand in this
matter, for He blessed the work more than you or I
could even ask or think. Charlie had

RETURNED FROM HIS WANDERINGS,

having had many experiences in which God always
spared his life. In one of these narrow escapes he was
almost killed. This put him in a hospital for several
months.

When I returned to L—— he was there, and by a
special appointment of God, He led me to Charlie's
home. His brother was anything but friendly to me
when I left a few months before, but now they were all
good friends.

That night Charlie and some others

CAME TO THE MERCY SEAT.

He was saved and seemed to do well for a few days when
he became convicted for holiness. This he could not get

because he had a brother in Chicago whom he would not forgive. However, on Sunday, after we had dismissed the meeting and had the prayer meeting, Charlie came back and the comrades

ASKED HIM TO SURRENDER.

He told a dream that he had. He saw a ball of fire circling around his head; then it burſted and he saw the angel sounding the trumpet and following that he saw the whole Salvation Army. His mother, who was also dealing with him, told how she had seen a ſtreak of divine fire come down near her while she was working. This frightened me, for I knew it was

THE JUDGMENT OF GOD.

I told them that Charlie should either get saved that night or go to hell. I then went to the penitent form and knelt in prayer. The comrades ſtood around him and sang " Mother's Prayers Have Followed Me " and " Liſten to Her Pleading." He

COULD STAND IT NO LONGER

but came and knelt at the mercy seat. He even then would not give up a grudge he had in his heart. When he refused, God seemed to ſtrike him as with a thunder bolt. He saw hell and heaven.

THEN GOD SAVED HIM

and after being under the power of God for nearly an hour behold old things had passed away and behold all things had become new.

Charlie is going to The Salvation Army Training College as soon as he can raise the money to buy uniforms and other things that he needs. We are now praying for his brothers.

6

Sweet, juicy and affecting words of the eloquent Denver
News when the Kiwanis Clubs came to town:

The strangers within our gates, coming under their
banners of Blue and White, symbols of Idealism and
Purity, are well worthy to hold the keys to this, the
Halfway House of the Continent. They are engaged
in a great undertaking.

They are raising a structure to the Known God which
all who love their fellows may worship without question.
Its cornerstone is Fair-dealing; its archstone is Charity,
which is Love. Its pillars are Comradeship, Service,
Tolerance, Helpfulness. Those who would view the
Kiva which Kiwanians are building must have their
mortal eyes opened, their vision cleansed, their minds
made responsive to what the building stands for, otherwise they are blind and cannot see it, much less enter it.
To appreciate the work being done the spirit must be
aroused in man. This temple is not being constructed
of dead brick and stone and of timber that must decay.
The material which we have in mind is of a different
character and, strange to state, it grows stronger with
the years and the added weight which it may be called
on to carry. It is a structure being built of good deeds
with humanity's trowel. The cement is not of blood
wrenched from the suffering of the weak and oppressed.
The bindery is all-embracing, delicately made of
generous deeds and the heart-beats of man toward his
fellow-man. Within it are rods of steel made of the
muscles of heroes. The spans are of the handclasps of
Kiwanians and the spans are not dead but living, ever-
expanding, having no limit to their reach.

In the Holy of Holies is an Altar to Childhood. It is
veiled with gossamer robes of Charity. It is for the one

who by the laws of Karma is born into the world with a handicap for which it cannot be held responsible. On that Altar grown man enters his heart purified to remove the handicap upon the child and give it a start in the world. When he enters the sacred place he becomes as a child himself, with the heart of a child, and it is good for him to be there.

The temple-builders are not of one nation or of one blood. They believe in Internationalism that does not take away the right kind of patriotism. They believe in the day " when man to man the world o'er brothers shall be and all that."

Within the temple they gather in a spirit of perfect equality. Their businesses and professions are many, but they are as one under the Kiwanis banner. They have come together to know one another better, to make life more cheerful, to give encouragement to the weak and faltering in a true spirit of fellowship and comradeship.

> Not that men are poor;
> All men know something of poverty.
> Not that men are wicked;
> Who can claim to be good?
> Not that men are ignorant;
> Who can boast that he is wise?
> But that men are strangers!

The international Convention of Kiwanis Clubs represents a power for good in this world that has lost in recent years several of its sociological props. We ask that Denver give to the Kiwanians this week what the Kiwanians would do as Kiwanians to one another, and to man his brother wherever the Kiwanian handclasp can reach.

7

From a letter addressed by the Rev. F. H. Rice, of the Liberal Church of Denver to the manufacturers of a favorite soft drink called Whistle:

In this day of Prohibition you have heard of many churches that have supplanted the communion wine with grape juice but we claim to be the first to use Whistle for this very important service.

At 11 A.M. last Sunday morning every member of the Liberal Church partook of Whistle as the Lord's Supper and during the ceremony five large Whistle signs and three linen banners were prominently displayed.

The purity, quality, and general excellence of your beverage well justify its being used in such a manner and we think that many others will follow our example.

8

From the letter-head of the same church:

DEPARTMENT OF BIBLE LITERATURE
Fred B. Keeler, *Chairman*

MOTHERS' CULTURE CLUB
Dr. L. Mary Morgan, M.D., *Instructor*

FATHERS' CULTURE CLUB
Elwood Hillis, *Instructor*

WOMEN'S DEPARTMENT
Mrs. A. C. Stevens

DEPARTMENT OF POLITICAL SCIENCE
Hon. Barney Haughey, D.U.R.
Clyde Robinson, M.R.S.
Dr. Jim Meyers, D.U.R.

DEPARTMENT OF PSYCHO-ANALYSIS
Dr. E. M. Ryman, M.D.
John Grattan, R.D.D.

LEGAL COMMITTEE
Hon. Bert Martin
Hon. C. M. Bice
Hon. Tom Herrington
Hon. Barney Haughey
Hon. Edwin N. Burdick

DEPARTMENT OF ANCIENT HISTORY
Frank Munroe

DEPARTMENT OF AMERICANIZATION
William A. Cloud, *Chairman*

DEPARTMENT OF SPIRITUAL EDUCATION
Dr. E. C. Porter, D.U.R., *Chairman*

CUSTODIAN OF SACRAMENTS
O. L. Smith

CUSTODIAN OF CHURCH HALL
Ed. Beyers

DEPARTMENT OF AMUSEMENTS
H. E. Ellison
Ben Ketchum

DEPARTMENT OF BASEBALL
Paul R. Felix

DEPARTMENT OF SCIENTIFIC DIET
Grace Bonnet, D.U.R., *Chairman*

DEPARTMENT OF CREATIVE CHEMISTRY
Henry Hefty, *Chairman*

DEPARTMENT OF METAPHYSICS
Prof. Frank D. Hines, *Chairman*

DEPARTMENT OF DANCING
Professor Petersen

DEPARTMENT OF NEW SCIENCES
Dr. B. Stosik, D.C., *Chairman*

DEPARTMENT OF CHRISTIAN PHILOSOPHY
William Ackerman, *Chairman*

DEPARTMENT OF TAX ADJUSTMENT
J. Stone, *Chairman*

CHILDREN'S DEPARTMENT (GIRLS)
Miss Margaret J. Gibson, M.R.R.

CHILDREN'S DEPARTMENT (BOYS)
Hon. J. Walter Wynn

DEPARTMENT OF LOGIC
W. E. Landau, D.U.R.

DEPARTMENT ORIGIN OF RELIGIONS
Sam Greene, Sr.

DEPARTMENT OF PHILOSOPHY
Hon. Halsey M. Rhodes

DEPARTMENT OF MUSIC
Hon. J. F. Bixby

DEPARTMENT OF ENGINEERING
E. C. Walker
Charles Harrison

DEPARTMENT OF CONSTRUCTION
A. G. Grissam

DEPARTMENT OF REAL ESTATE
Victor R. Olmstead

DEPARTMENT OF "TRUTH-SEEKER"
Garrie P. Bishop

DEPARTMENT OF ORIGIN THEOSOPHY
Minnie May Bixler

9

Heroic renunciation of the editor of the eminent Boulder *News-Herald*:

Politicians try to punish editors who will not sacrifice convictions for commercialism. Because the state Republican organization is controlled by the Ku Klux Klan, the *News-Herald* will not be given any part of the contract to publish initiated and referred measures in Boulder county. We should rather lose money for the sake of a principle than take money at the expense of our conscientious beliefs.

10

Law-making by the *Polizei* in Denver, as reported by the patriotic *Post*:

Chief of Police Candlish issued an edict Thursday forbidding white women or white girls being in the employ of Greek, Japanese, Chinese, Mexican or Negro restaurants, candy stores or other places of business. It is estimated more than 100 white women are now working in such places. The chief did not promise to find jobs for them. " I'm not going to allow any white girl to be in the employ of these people," he said.

11

Condition of the customers of optimistic Colorado realtors, as reported by a correspondent of the La Junta *Tribune*:

The general talk of the country is dry weather and short grass, and who will (or who can) move first. We have stolen from one another until stealing is no longer a paying business, and we can't all be bootleggers. Besides, corn is so poor it won't make a gallon an acre, and so God only knows what is to become of us.

12

Comparative justice in the back country, as reported by the eminent Denver *Post*:

G. E. Robkey, of Limon, Colo., a deacon in the Methodist church there, was fined $10 and costs, a total of $35, for tying strings of tin cans to horses' and mules' tails and causing them to run in fright until exhausted, according to Humane Officer W. V. Truett, who returned to Denver Saturday after prosecuting the case. The deacon's hired man, R. R. Grundy, also was fined $35 and was sentenced to jail for thirty days because the court held he was more guilty than the deacon. He is alleged to have tied the cans on the strings so the deacon could tie them on the tails.

13

High words of the Hon. William E. Sweet, A.B., ΦKΨ, Governor of Colorado:

It is my belief that the foreign secretaries of the Young Men's Christian Association are better acquainted with industrial, social, political and religious movements which are taking place in foreign lands than any other persons, *not excepting the representatives of our government.* The type of men which the Association sends abroad for foreign service is of the very highest. They are leaders in every sense of the word.

14

Complex but affecting instructions to patriotic school children prepared by the talented Alwin D. Farrior, of Walsenburg, director of the Americanism Commission of the American Legion:

After the colors are in position, the Trumpeter, if the school has one, will blow "To the Colors." Then the Captain, or teacher, gives the command: "Right Hand Salute." This is done by raising the right hand smartly till the tip of the forefinger touches the lower part of the headdress (if uncovered, the forehead above the right eye), thumb and fingers extended and joined, palm to the left, forearm inclined at about 45 degrees, hand and wrist straight. Then drop the hand smartly by the side. Always look toward the colors when saluting them. In the grade schools this may be followed by an additional salute: " We give our hands, our heads and our hearts to our country and to our flag." In giving this part of the salute raise both hands toward the flag immediately after the right hand salute has been completed. Then drop left hand to side and raise right hand to forehead. Then place right hand on heart, and as the words " to our flag " are spoken, advance the right foot and point with the right hand to the flag.

15

Contribution to Law Enforcement by the Hon. Sam E. Thomas, sheriff of Pueblo, as reported by the Pueblo *Chieftain*:

The sheriff is considering steps to frustrate the imbiber of spirits who pours all the evidence down his throat, smashes the bottle and then laughs at the officers. Raiding officers will have, in addition to their side artillery, a stomach pump. The purpose of this instrument will not be to revive the victims. Its application will be the recovery of hastily gulped evidence, and if the object of the assault survives he will be confronted with a charge of illegal possession.

CONNECTICUT

1

Theological news note from the free imperial city of Middletown, the seat of Wesleyan University, the Berkeley Divinity School and the Connecticut State Hospital for the Insane:

The Rev. Minard Le G. Porter, pastor of the Methodist Church at Long Hill, near Middletown, has won the Bible Marathon by reading the New Testament in thirteen hours. Commencing shortly before midnight, he kept reading without interruption save for a few minutes to take nourishment.

2

Effects of the Higher Learning at Yale, as revealed by the answers to a questionnaire submitted to the students there:

Favorite character in world history: Napoleon, 181; Cleopatra, 7; Jeanne d'Arc, 7; Woodrow Wilson, 7; Socrates, 5; Jesus Christ, 4; Mussolini, 3.

Favorite prose author: Stevenson, 24; Dumas, 22; Sabatini, 11; Anatole France, 5; Cabell, 5; Bernard Shaw, 4.

Favorite magazine: Saturday Evening Post, 94; *Atlantic Monthly,* 24; *New Republic,* 3; *Times Current History,* 3.

Favorite political party: Republican, 304; Democratic, 84; none, 22; Independent, 3.

34

Biggest world figure of today : Coolidge, 52; Dawes, 32; Mussolini, 3; Prince of Wales, 24; J. P. Morgan, 15; Einstein, 3; Bernard Shaw, 3.

What subject would you like to see added to the curriculum : Elocution and Public Speaking, 24; Business course, 8; Diplomacy, 7; Drama, 4.

3

Appeal to the music-lovers of Yale in an advertisement in the *Yale Daily News :*

BESSIE SMITH

Bessie Smith, the Babe Ruth of all blues singers, comes to bat now with " Nobody in Town Can Bake a Sweet Jelly Roll Like Mine." She's blued about her troubles, she's blued about her men, she's blued about her baby, and now she blues again. If she bakes a jelly roll as well as she sings about it—no wonder everybody wants to cut himself a piece of cake!

Roll that record over. What's this Bessie says? Oh, yes, " If You Don't, I Know Who Will." Well, Bessie, after hearing this we will.

Released at
WHITLOCK'S
today.

4

Mature conclusion of the Hon. William J. O'Brien, a favorite publicist of New Haven:

Woodrow Wilson is the greatest statesman the world has as yet produced.

5

The clean, wholesome amusement of Christian business men, as reported by the distinguished New Haven *Register*:

Four hundred members of the Rotary Club, who Rolls-Royced and Forded to the McAlpin Hotel, New York, last week for the club's weekly luncheon, looked at Ned Wayburn and listened to him tell how he picks chorus beauties that completely satisfy the exacting demands of Ziegfeld and other producers. The members were extremely attentive.

" A girl's throat is the same circumference as the calf of her leg," confided Wayburn. . . . He explained the close scrutiny that a girl endures when applying for a position in the merry-merry. It is necessary to " look right through " the applicant, deciding at a glance whether she has the needed symmetry of body. . . . The age of the applicant is told by looking at the back of her hand. . . .

The members all pronounced the talk as having been highly educational. They passed out of the dining room singing, " Hello, Hello, Hello " with full chorusian gestures, and returned to their offices to look at the backs of their stenographers' hands.

6

Pedagogical dictum of Prof. Dr. William Lyon Phelps, of Yale, quoted in the advertising of the Moody Bible Institute:

Everyone who has a thorough knowledge of the Bible may truly be called educated; and no other learning or culture, no matter how extensive or elegant, can form a proper substitute.

7

Dispatch from Middletown:

Asserting that there is technically no such thing as a highball, Professor Karl P. Harrington, head of the Latin department at Wesleyan, has asked for the suppression of the college song, "Drink a Highball at Nightfall."

8

From an address by the Rev. Frederick W. Adams, D.D., of Springfield, Mass., to the Hartford Rotary Club:

If Mark Twain were alive today he would be a Rotarian.

9

Début of a new crime in the land of Blue Laws, as reported by the Waterbury *Republican:*

Amelia Moses, eighteen, was arrested yesterday by Lieutenants Timothy Hickey and Milton MacMullen of the Detective Bureau, charged with *being in danger of falling into vice*.

10

From the platform of the new board of editors of the *Yale News:*

The Eighteenth Amendment should be strictly enforced throughout the university.
Compulsory chapel should be retained.
There should be a course on the Bible as literature.
There should be a course in dramatic art.

11

Obiter dictum of Maltbie, J., of the Superior Court of Hartford:

The man who buys liquor is an enemy of society . . . and a traitor to his country.

12

Decision of the learned Aubrey, J., of the City Court of Meriden, in Dziekiela vs. Kama, an action for slander on the ground that the defendant called the plaintiff a drunkard:

An oral charge of drunkardness is not actionable *per se* unless it charges a crime, or unless it is coupled with some business in which drunkardness is a disqualification. Our practice requires that oral words, to be actionable in themselves, must either charge an offense which upon conviction would call for an infamous punishment or an offense which involves moral turpitude. It goes without saying that drunkardness does not call for an infamous punishment and in a refined sense, drunkardness in the sense of intoxication is not of itself made a misdemeanor or crime in this State. The gravamen of the offense lies in being found intoxicated. Counsel suggests that since the enactment of the Eighteenth Amendment and the enforcement laws supposed to carry the same into effect, drunkardness has become a crime involving moral turpitude. But the penalty for intoxication still remains unchanged and we cannot find that this claim is well founded either in law or in fact.

DELAWARE

I

Beneficent influence of Prohibition in lower Delaware, as revealed in a dispatch from the rising town of Wyoming to the eminent Wilmington *News*:

Since the enactment of Federal and State Prohibition laws . . . not only boys of high school age, but girls and other younger children, frequently are seen under the influence of the prohibited liquor. . . . Boys have been seen staggering on the streets, and asleep at their desks.

DISTRICT OF COLUMBIA

I

From an article in the *Georgetown Law Journal* on the junket of the American Bar Association to London, by Noel F. Regis, A.B., A.M., LL.B., Ph.D., member of the faculty of philosophy in the Catholic University of America, professor of Roman jurisprudence and medieval institutions in the Georgetown University Law School, and professor of economics in Georgetown College:

> The fraternal foregathering of the twin peoples who are proud to owe allegiance to the Lady of the Common Law was really one of the greatest movements in the development of Anglo-Saxon civilization, comparable only in its influence, extent and effect to the Crusades, racial migrations, colonization of America, and American participation in the late war. This is not an exaggerated statement. . . .

2

From a public bull by the Hon. James John Davis, director-general of the Loyal Order of Moose and Secretary of Labor in the Cabinet of Mr. Coolidge:

> There should be a fourth R added to the modern school course. With reading, 'riting and 'rithmetic you should put religion, for if you are going to make a success of life in the American way you must have the fourth R.

3

Decay of the Higher Morality in the House of Representatives, as reported by the *Congressional Record*:

Mr. CLARK of Florida. Mr. Speaker, I desire to ask unanimous consent that I may proceed for one minute on a matter of great interest to the House.

The SPEAKER. The gentleman from Florida asks unanimous consent to proceed for one minute. Is there objection?

There was no objection.

Mr. CLARK of Florida. Mr. Speaker, while this House seems to be in the way of liberalization, I want to suggest that for a long time—and I am not so old, either —there has been a rule, as I understand, which forbids Members of Congress having a couch or lounge or something on which they might rest for a few minutes in their offices if they desire to do so. That I regard as a reflection on the integrity and the honor of the membership of the House, and I wanted to raise this question now, Mr. Speaker, in order that the commission having charge of that building might take into consideration the question of allowing the Members who desired it the privilege of having some convenience there if they desire to rest for a few moments some time during the day. [*Applause.*]

4

From a church notice in the Washington *News*:

E. Hez Swem, pastor of the Centennial Baptist Church, will preach on " Why a Man Threw a Large Dinner Dish and a Chicken Out of a Window." He calls it Summer Story No. 1.

5

Specimen of current Washington correspondence, from the Indianapolis *Star*:

Another pleasant thing about the President is his nice, ſtraight legs. Not a trace of curvature, of knocking of the knees, of bumps or hollows, mars his ambulatory equipment. He is as ſtraight and upright as a sapling, fashioned so slenderly, young, and so fair. His legs look beſt in black, his favorite hue. He is scrupulously pressed and valeted, juſt out of the bandbox effeƈt. Gay tints in neckwear are not to the presidential taſte. He likes black scarfs brocaded in white or silver, held faſt by a modeſt little pearl or diamond, neat but not gaudy.

6

Progress of the New Jurisprudence in the shadow of the Washington monument, as reported by the celebrated Washington *Poſt*:

Police early today raided the premises at 345 Pennsylvania Avenue northweſt, and arreſted fifteen Chinamen on charges of playing mah-jong, in the firſt raid of this kind in Washington.

7

How the Department of Agriculture earns its $150,000,-000 a year, from page 9 of Farmers' Bulletin No. 1099:

In order to determine whether, from the money ſtandpoint, it is cheaper to wash by hand or to buy and operate a washing machine, the coſt of the two methods may be reckoned as follows: Divide the coſt of the machine by the number of years it will probably be used. To the result add the coſt of operation (about

5 cents an hour multiplied by the number of hours it will be used in a year, plus about $1.50 per year for oil and minor repairs). To reckon the cost of hand work, calculate the amount paid a laundress during the year for actual washing (not starching and ironing) and add the yearly cost of any meals and car fare given her; or, if no laundress is hired, multiply the number of hours you give to this work yearly by the price which a laundress receives per hour in your neighborhood.

8

Duties of the 100% American, as set forth in a Federal Citizenship Textbook issued by the Department of Labor:

> We must respect those above us. It pays. Be loyal to your employer. Don't be fooled by wrong talk. Speak well of your bosses to other workmen.

9

Effects of the Law Enforcement campaign under the shadow of the White House, as reported by the Washington *Daily News:*

> Gin, synthetic of course, which cost $7 a short quart in Washington three years ago, has gradually slid down the scale to three and four. Some is even lower. Whiskeys which brought from $12 to $20 are now from $6 to $10.

10

More evidence in the same direction from the same great moral and intellectual newspaper:

> The police have issued a report showing that arrests for drunkenness in the District have increased 121%

since 1910. During this period the population grew
32.17%. Arrests for driving automobiles while drunk
have increased 850.94% since 1918.

11

Picture of democratic government in the one hundred
and thirty-ninth year of the Republic, from a speech in the
Senate by the Hon. James Thomas Heflin, of Alabama:

The Federal departments here are honeycombed with
crooks and gorged with grafters.

12

High words of the Rev. Burke Culpepper, at Mount
Vernon Place Methodist Episcopal Church South:

Dancing is a divorce feeder. It is heathen, animalistic
and damnable. It results in spiritual paralysis. It de-
grades womanhood and manhood. Now is the time to
say plainly that it is one of the most pernicious of all
modern customs.

13

Report of a modern miracle from the Washington *Herald*:

The odor of perfume was wafted through Centennial
Baptist Church, Seventh and I Streets, Northeast, last
night, as the Rev. E. Hez Swem, emphasizing a vigorous sermon, waved a scented handkerchief at his
congregation.

"Want to smell it?" he asked. "It's perfume, and
it came from the Lord above."

Inspiration for a message had come to him when a
feminine member of his flock gave him a bottle of

perfume, the Rev. Mr. Swem said. He really wanted
some perfume, and God knew he wanted it and gave it
to him through this good woman, he said.

14

From a public bull by the Board of Temperance, Prohibition and Public Morals of the Methodist Episcopal
Church:

> No representative body in the world surpasses the
> American Congress in intelligence or character.

15

First fruits of Education Week in Washington, from an
address to the students of the Eastern High School by
Dr. Kate Waller Barrett, national chairman of the Congress of Mothers and Parent-Teacher Associations:

> I am a Democrat and I voted for Davis, but I thank
> God President Coolidge was reëlected and I want to
> pledge every girl in this school never to let a word of
> criticism of Mr. Coolidge or of the government pass
> her lips during the four years he will be in office.

16

From a dispatch from the same city to the eminent New
York *World*:

> Two factions of the District of Columbia Chapter of
> the United Daughters of the Confederacy almost
> reached the hair-pulling stage in Memorial Confederate
> Hall, near the Department of Justice, this afternoon.
> Shrieks rent the air in that fashionable neighborhood
> and some one called the police. Private Baxter, a

Negro, responded. His appearance caused a fresh outbreak, and the irate women turned on him and ordered a quick retreat. He escaped.

17

Contribution to a new Gesta Romanorum by the current *Hofprediger*, as reported by the Washington *Herald*:

Jiggs, hen-pecked husband of Maggie, one of the comic strips appearing in the Washington *Herald*, served as an example in the sermon yesterday at the First Congregational Church. The Rev. Jason Noble Pierce, pastor of the church, speaking of the unhappiness of the rich, said: "Money does not always bring happiness. Mr. Jiggs knows this. Of course you all know Jiggs of the 'Bringing Up Father' cartoon. Recently Jiggs lost his fortune. Sitting on the steps of the pretentious residence from which he had just been evicted, Jiggs remarked, 'Oh well. You got to be poor to be happy anyway!' And that's the truth."

President and Mrs. Coolidge were among the congregation.

18

Stealthy approach of the Pope to the White House, as described by one of the leading Washington dailies:

A fragment of the bone of the right arm of St. Francis Xavier, known for his miracles in the Far East, will be exhibited tonight at the Church of St. Francis Xavier, Twenty-seventh and Pennsylvania avenue. The Rev. Joseph V. Buckley, pastor of the church, said that each night after the novena the relic will be venerated. "Since we have had the relic in the church," Father Buckley declared today, "we have had a remarkable cure reported. A boy in the parish was suffering with double mastoids and doctors gave up all hope for him. He touched the relic and now the boy is cured. There is no trace of the mastoids."

FLORIDA

Appearance of a new and fantastic heresy in the swamps behind Miami and Palm Beach, as reported by an alert correspondent of the Florida *Baptist Witness:*

I am not seeking a controversy, but would like to say that the custom that some Baptist churches have fallen into of oyster crackers and cubes of bakers' bread in the Lord's Supper is to my mind unscriptural and a digression from our Master's example and Apostolic usage.

2

How the Fourteenth Amendment is enforced among the Nordic Blond Baptists of rural Florida, as reported by the *Florida Sentinel,* an eminent Aframerican print of Jacksonville:

WARNING TO NEGRO TOURISTS

Those who have automobiles want to exercise more caution when driving over the State. The small villages and towns are still far from civilized and at every opportunity give their savagery full play. The Negro who drives a Ford gets by no better than one who drives a Lincoln. Every one must pay a toll for driving through these small white settlements. You don't have to speed. If you roll along at the rate of four miles an hour, if you happen to be the least colored it is sufficient

48

reason to hold you up and take from you a batch of your cold cash, and on top of that be rough-necked by a man whose nickel-faced badge is his only protection against the charge of highway robbery.

If you want to get abused be thoughtless enough to get short of gas near one of these village filling-stations. You are as likely as not to be arrested on a charge of car stealing and be detained in jail without even a chance of getting a hearing within a week.

The little country court is worse than the speed cop, so there you are. The country judge and speed cop must depend on those they victimize for their support. The town itself may not afford enough to keep up a razor-back hog. You can readily see how profitable it is to feed on Negro tourists, who may rest assured that the more respectable they look the more impressive will be the degradation heaped upon them by the cop and the trial court.

Don't take a chance against a backwoods speed-cop and court.

Don't leave your city unless you are certain you have enough gas to carry you to the next city.

Don't stop at the village filling-stations.

Don't buy sodas, cigars or lunches along the path of your trip.

Don't be hard-headed and get the experience of thousands of your fellow autoists who are just as careful to observe the law as you.

3

Good works of a soulless corporation in the wilds of Florida, as reported by the Clermont *Press:*

Solicited by E. C. Pemberton for aid in the building of the new Baptist Church, the Standard Oil representative stated that they had no funds for that purpose, but would see what they could do. This week there arrived at the depot, freight prepaid, a three-burner oil stove and a heater, compliments of the company. The Baptist people appreciate very much this gift.

4

Warning to potential evil-doers in Miami, as described by the esteemed *Herald* of that city:

A small monument made a mysterious appearance on S. E. First Street on the sidewalk near the Urmey Hotel, early yesterday morning. An inscription on one side of the monument reads: " On this spot a few years ago a white man was found who had been tarred and feathered because he preached social equality to Negroes." On another side were the words: " If you are a reckless Negro or a White man who believes in social equality, be advised Dade county don't need you." The monument had not been removed last night.

5

Advertisement of a Christian business man in the eminent Tampa *Tribune:*

THE DUNCAN CLEANING COMPANY

1215 *Florida Ave.*

Will open their place of business with a religious service conducted by Rev. G. S. Roberts, Dr. A. M. Bennett, Rev. J. L. Irvin and Rev. R. L. Allen.
Wednesday. . . . . 9 *o'Clock A. M.*
Music program will be arranged by

Mrs. L. H. Jones

Piano furnished by

M. L. PRICE MUSIC COMPANY
Decoration by TAMPA FLORAL COMPANY
EVERYBODY WELCOME——EVERYBODY INVITED

We will have the nicest, neatest, cleanest and best cleaning and pressing establishment in the city.

M. A. DUNCAN, *Mgr.*

6

Recreation among the master-minds of Tampa, as described by the esteemed *Tribune:*

Members of the Exchange Club at Monday's luncheon were forced to essay the rôle of amateur sword swallowers and eat with their knives. Those who showed the white feather by reaching for a fork or a spoon were fined 25 cents for the offense, about $5 being raised in this manner, to be added to the club's publicity fund for use at the national convention at Nashville, Tenn. The luncheon included cantaloupe a la mode, besides such edibles as stewed chicken and other items difficult to manage with a knife alone.

7

One year's doings of a Christian business man in Florida, as reported to *Collier's Weekly* by Mr. L. F. Vaught, of the up-and-coming town of Bradentown:

Played tennis fifty times.
Went fishing twice.
Went hunting five times.
Made ten trips from city.
Performed in five shows and engaged in thirty rehearsals.

Elected church lay leader, supervising and planning all activities of laymen in the church.

Attended church services 125 times.

Made fifteen public addresses.

Led in ten religious services.

Attended choir practice twenty-five times.

Elected district lay leader with jurisdiction over twenty charges.

Appointed chairman educational fund and chairman of lay committee on centenary fund with the same jurisdiction as above.

Sang fifteen solos.

Taught Sunday-school class six times.

Played two ball games

Elected president of the Wesley Federation with jurisdiction over about six thousand classes.

Served one week on the jury.

Elected president of an adult Bible class and adult superintendent in a Sunday-school of about six hundred members.

Attended 135 special meetings.

Helped to take a religious census of the city.

Elected vice president of the Business Men's Evangelistic Club.

Elected chairman Board of Trustees of Public Schools.

8

Observations along the American Riviera by the Rev. Robert T. Wightman, a visiting divine from New Jersey:

Nowhere in this country is there a parallel for conditions that exist in Florida. . . . Some of the biggest hotels shun married couples as their guests, preferring single men and women. Liquor is unrestricted and gambling dens are wide open. Monte Carlo is put in the shade. . . . Any wishing to go to hell can find greased planks a-plenty. . . . Law officers wink at all infractions and reprimands are followed by apologies.

GEORGIA

From a parishioner's tribute to the Rev. Dr. R. H.
Singleton, deceased, late pastor of Big Bethel African
M. E. Church, Atlanta:

He was a splendid educator and a pulpit orator, if you
please. To comment from all sources, he was thrilled
with the spirit and the Holy Fire. In spite of the handi-
caps he delivered the goods so plain that a child could
understand his illustration. He solved the problem of
the human soul, sadly, not knowing on that sad Sunday
morning that he was preaching his own funeral from one
of the dearest appeals sent out into the heart of man and
illustrations that ever fell from the lips of human being
since the Christian world. Awakened on the following
Monday morning early, before the break of day, everybody was spell bound and shocked to pieces to know the
voice of our race ambassador had stilled forever. Ex-
clusively he was a spokesman of his people and a friend
to the widows and poor orphan children. To excuse
none, he has made a record; no man can write the
history for the uplift of fallen humanity. He planned
church co-operations, put ideals over where other men
failed and made ends meet in the circle of worth-while.
He brought wonders to pass. To magnify the peace
and good will among men on earth, he was a charming
hero, a dying statesman with a bright determination to
go ahead and face the crisis. In spite of the appoint-

ments and disappointments he advanced and stood his ground upon a platform and was unshaken by man. He taught the people the power of having faith in God. He was an American one hundred per cent and citizen of the world whose popularity had won greater influence among the leading citizens of the city than any one had ever thought to dream for. Not only was he a soldier in the Christian warfare but he was a conqueror and leader of men who need no introduction. He was known by his good works, a son of the family and wonderful progress of activities. He demonstrated that true liberty under race men's influence might be understood the world over. But to honor him, we give credit to a Christian gentleman, the ambassador gifted from God, the honest leader in public affairs, who served his people and dealt with the currents on a fifty-fifty basis. As a majority he was a masterpiece of an extraordinary reputation, backed up with a wholesome culture and keen humor and merit the world will live long to forget.

2

Progress of the heretic hunt in the capital of the Invisible Empire and Coca Cola, as reported by the Associated Press from Atlanta:

In a sermon preached last night at the Central Baptist Church, the Rev. W. L. Hambrick, the pastor, severely scored President Coolidge for having "placed God third" in a radio address to Boy Scouts. "During the World War," said Dr. Hambrick, "we justly criticized and condemned the Kaiser for referring to God as secondary—' me und Gott '—but last Friday our own President took the liberty of moving God down a step further and put Him in third place. In his radio address to the Boy Scouts he urged them to reverence first nature, second law, third God. It is very unfortunate that our President should have been so careless with his thoughts and words, for in so doing, in my judgment, he has not only dishonored the office he holds, but that God we worship and serve. I think it is a shame on our Nation and a slur on Christianity."

3

The gay life in the same great city, as described by the Society Editor of the *Journal:*

One of the most unique, as well as one of the most enjoyable events ever given in Atlanta was the dinner Friday evening at the Piedmont Driving Club at which Mr. Wilmer Moore, chairman of the board of deacons of the North Avenue Presbyterian Church, entertained in honor of the Rev. Richard Orme Flinn, pastor of the church.

Invited to meet the pastor were the elders and deacons of the church and in especial compliment to these guests the table was arranged with many little groups of Biblical figures.

Adam and Eve, made of gum drops, were seen seated under a tiny apple tree, the bright red apples being represented by cranberries, and the old serpent, made of raisins, was seen very near them.

Moses was shown, made of peanuts, in a grapefruit rind basket placed in the bulrushes, with Pharaoh's daughter, a lollipop.

At the places of the pastor and the elders were tiny Bibles, made of candy, with a quotation in the tiniest of letters, and the bookmarks were sprays of rosebuds.

4

Progress of Fundamentalism in bucolic Georgia, as revealed by a press dispatch from the State capital:

During a debate in the Legislature on a measure to allow counties, school districts, or municipalities to establish and maintain public libraries, either by taxation or by donations, Representative Hal Wimberly, of Laurens county, made a speech against the bill. According to Mr. Wimberly there are only three books worth reading in the world—the Bible, the hymnbook and the almanac. " Those three are enough for anyone," said the Laurens representative. " Read the Bible. It teaches you how to act. Read the hymnbook. It contains the finest poetry ever written. Read the almanac. It shows you how to figure out what the weather will be. There isn't another book that is necessary for anyone to read and therefore I am opposed to all libraries."

The measure failed to pass. The vote on agreeing to the favorable report of the committee was 57 for and 63 against.

5

From a public address by Prof. Wesley Peacock, described by the eminent *Georgian* as " a well-known educator ":

Success in business is no criterion for genius. Success socially ought to be, and usually is, for geniuses are usually, according to the case histories of 643 of them and more on record, well developed physically and socially, are good sports, and are leaders in public speaking, histrionics, debating and organization. They make good newspaper reporters and feature writers.

6

Dreadful effects of pedagogical Bolshevism among the Georgia crackers, as described by the patriotic Atlanta *Georgian:*

Instead of censoring school books so severely, we should censor school teachers. Many a man or woman who is a good teacher should never be permitted to teach. Years ago a young man was chosen as principal of a large school in a country town. He was a university graduate and well equipped with a normal-school training besides. His conduct was without reproach. His manner was genial and his discipline was firm. His pupils were devoted to him, and his patrons congratulated themselves upon having secured his services. Then one day a good little widow who had a son in the senior class of the high school discovered that he was a Simonpure atheist, with pronounced political tendencies toward blood and anarchy! There was a great hue and cry when the parents of that town tapped their sons and daughters and tested their views concerning life, love, religion and morals. The Decalogue was gone; the Scriptures had been wiped out of them; and the last one of them had been well instructed in the most advanced doctrines of Socialism. The teacher left town between suns, but the mischief had been done. The members of that senior class have never settled down into good, substantial, bench-legged, bull-dog citizens. Some of them have had criminal careers.

7

Rise of literary passion among the Atlanta Fundamentalists, as reported by another of the city's public prints:

THE SUSANNAH SPOT LIGHT

The Susannah Wesley class of the Druid Hills
Methodist Sunday-school is getting out a snappy little
sheet under the above caption. The editor is Mrs.
C. A. Mauck, who is also corresponding secretary of the
Federated Church Women of Georgia, with Mrs. J. V.
Hodges as assistant editor.

The spirit of the *Spot Light* is expressed in the following rhyme by Miss Willis Terry:

BE A BOOSTER

Things are the finest at Druid Hills.
Susannah's the kindest at Druid Hills.
Folks are the truest, and slackers the fewest;
The atmosphere the purest at Druid Hills.

Folks do look neatest at Druid Hills.
The music is sweetest at Druid Hills.
Faces are the brightest, hearts beat the lightest.
For folks act the whitest at Druid Hills.

8

Specimen of the late Georgian rococo style from a set of
resolutions adopted by the gifted board of directors of the
Georgia Railroad and Banking Company, of Augusta:

For some good reason, we know not why, like the
lightning's blast shivers a monarch of the forest in the
fullness of its glory before the measured limit of its

years of useful service by man's reckoning had come, so death struck Jacob Phinizy, a noted and distinguished figure in our midst, because of his boldness, prominence and greatness perhaps, and hid him from our eyes and communion, and crumbled the proud and stalwart proportions of his brain, courage and power into the dust of humanity, which await alike the inevitable of the high and lofty, as well as those of simple and low estate, and which encompasses, encrusts and decays departed mankind, leaving the heritage of his life and character to us left behind.

9

Proud boasts of the estimable Atlanta *Constitution:*

Georgia produces enough fine apples each year for every man, woman and child in the State to have two bushels.

Georgia's sanitarium for the insane has had for the past year every bed occupied and many waiting to be taken in.

10

Sign posted on a public road in South Georgia:

noTiS

Trespaser's will be persekuted to the full extent of 2 mongral dogs which ain't never been overly soshibil with strangers and 1 dubble barrel shot gun which ain't loaded with no sofy pillers. Dam if I ain't tired of this hel raisin on my proputy.

11

Miraculous work of the Holy Spirit at Arlington, as reported in a special dispatch to the Fort Worth (Texas) *Star-Telegram:*

The boll weevil hasn't touched the seven acres set aside here for the Lord.

Furthermore, the seven farmers who consecrated an acre each to the church are prospering in everything they have planted.

In contrast to their flourishing farms is the devastation that has been wrought everywhere in this section by the boll weevil. Cotton has been eaten up bodily and almost without exception the only farmers near Arlington who will make money this year are the seven who set aside an acre each for God's work.

At the opening of Spring, the Rev. H. M. Melton, pastor of the Bluffton Baptist Church, near here, asked each farmer in his church to stake off one acre and give the proceeds to the church.

Seven pledged themselves to do this and signed the following agreement: " We, the undersigned farmer members of the Bluffton Baptist Church, do agree to stake off, plant, cultivate, and harvest one acre of our respective farms. The product of said acre, when in marketable condition, is to be turned over to a committee appointed by the church to receive and sell, and the proceeds of said acre to be used in the work of the Lord."

Through the acres devoted to the Lord, the church expects to raise money enough to pay its pastor's salary.

IDAHO

I

Progress of Law Enforcement and the New Jurisprudence in Idaho, as reported by the American Civil Liberties Union:

Governor C. C. Moore is endeavoring to ſtrengthen the State Criminal Syndicalism Aᨘ by asking the legislature to change the definition of sabotage to cover, among other things, " slowing down work on produᨘion," " work done in an improper manner," " improper use of materials " and " loitering at work."

2

Rise of sportsmanship among the Chriſtians of the Snake river country, as reported by the Weiser *American:*

Considerable excitement was occasioned at the Chriſtian church laſt Sunday morning. It was not a case for the fire department this time, but a riot call was sent in for the sheriff. When the sheriff arrived he could find nothing but some people who were very shocked and mortified at the aᨘions of the paſtor, who loſt his temper so much that he pushed a lady out of the door. Moſt of the congregation deplore an aᨘion of this kind, especially at a public meeting.

3

The marvels of science in rural Idaho, as reported by the eminent Teton Valley *News:*

Dr. Martin informs us that he has invested in a horoscope for the X-ray machine at the County Hospital. This enables the surgeon to look directly at the part of the body operated on.

ILLINOIS

1

The Higher Learning at the eminent University of Illinois, as reported by the Chicago *Tribune:*

William R. Carroll of the University of Utah was appointed professor of swine husbandry at the University of Illinois yesterday. Prof. Carroll will take his chair on Feb. 1, 1925.

2

Æsthetic note from the distinguished *Daily Review-Atlas* of Monmouth:

AUCTION——SATURDAY——2 P.M.

Some of the pictures of the late Miss Agnes Strang, who taught art here for nearly 25 years. Among them are:

"Sunset on Lake George, New York"

This is said to be the prettiest lake east of the Allegheny mountains. I saw it 26 years ago. It is beautiful. There is a possibility that next year the convention of the U. P. Young People will meet there.

Also some household goods.

D. J. STRANG.

3

Specimen advertisements from the *Moody Bible Institute Monthly* of Chicago:

ROLLING MILL EVANGELIST. FORMERLY ROLLING MILL manager. Open for engagements. Geo. W. Jacoby, Primos, Pa., Box 34.

REV. CHARLES E. DRIVER. SAFE, CONSTRUCTIVE evangelism. Former Pastor. Experienced evangelist. Eminently successful. Finest Testimonials. Write for open dates. Palmyra, N.Y.

EVANGELIST AND BIBLE TEACHER, JONAS VUKER, WITH 28 years' experience as a pastor-evangelist and Bible teacher, has some open dates for evangelistic meetings or Bible Conferences, single or union meetings. For dates, references, etc., address Springfield, Ohio, R.D.10.

LADY EVANGELIST, TRAINED IN ALL BRANCHES OF evangelistic work. Conducts own singing and chorus work. Assist pastor or take full charge of revival meeting. Teaching or pulpit supply. Terms reasonable. Box L. M., Moody Monthly.

BIBLES REPAIRED OR REBOUND AT A REASONABLE PRICE. Satisfaction guaranteed. E. Holmgren Book Bindery, Coloma, Mich.

SEND YOUR DOLLAR TODAY AND HELP TRAIN A BRIGHT Chinese boy to become a preacher to his own people. God will bless you. All remittances acknowledged. Personal checks acceptable. (China postage five cents.) Rev. H.G. Miller, Wuchow, Kwangsi, China.

WANTED—NAMES AND ADDRESSES OF CHRISTIAN PEOple who will promise to pray for a revival to sweep over Arizona. Robert McMurdo, Peoria, Ariz.

$250,000 IN UNREAL MONEY. 250 TEN DOLLAR BILLS with Gospel Message on reverse side, 25c. Also free samples of other novelties. Gospel Co., Stapleton, N.Y.

4

From the application for membership in the Order of Bookfellows, an organization of Chicago literati:

Recognizing the solemnity of this step, I do hereby pledge myself to be a true and loyal Bookfellow, to cherish the good in literature and strive to make it my own, to revere genius, to guard and defend the truth, *to be kindly and tolerant toward those who think as I do,* and to maintain the ancient traditions *whenever I agree with them.*

5

Progress of Christian work among Chicago total immersionists, as reported by the estimable *Tribune:*

" Women defy classification," said the Rev. H. R. Griffin, pastor of the Rogers Park Baptist Church, Hilldale and Greenleaf avenues, after he had exhibited five types of girls to his audience. His subject was " The Kind of Girl to Marry." Each one of the young women stepped into a framework of flowers and tissue paper lattice work which had been arranged in the front of the church over the baptistry, while a spotlight was turned on.

6

Contribution of the *Herald and Examiner* to the same shining record:

Religious enterprises do not necessarily require a somber garb and unbending mien. At least that is the philosophy of the Loyal Fellows' Bible class of the Immanuel Baptist Church. They are going to try and win the all-Chicago Bible class attendance contest in the spirit of a jolly frolic. To that end they have divided

their class of forty members into the "Sparkplugs,"
"Sassy Susies" and "Heebie Jeebies." Don Cun-
ningham will be "Barney Google" for the "Sparkplugs." He will be assisted by Vincent Masten and
H. S. Ruppel as "Sunshine" and "Rudy." For the
"Sassy Susies," T. G. Murray will be the "Colonel"
and William Robinson "chief stable boy." The
"Heebie Jeebies" will be led by "Jack" Alberts as
"the jockey."

7

How captains of industry in the faubourgs of Chicago
relax from the strains of Service, as reported by the
patriotic Southtown *Economist:*

Englewood Kiwanians . . . starred in the gentle art of
rolling popcorn balls with their noses.

8

The rewards of a 100% American artiste among the
Chicago illuminati, as described by a press-sheet issued
by the publicist of Mme. Bernice de Pasquali, the opera
singer:

Mme. de Pasquali is a Daughter of the American
Revolution. Her ancestry dates back to the Lovells
and Dills of *Mayflower* times. . . . Recently in Chicago
she was made an Honorary Elk.

9

From a pious reader of the eminent Chicago *Tribune:*

If the Secretary of Agriculture will grip the fact that
God controls our agriculture it would not be such a
matter of constant concern to the department. Why is
the boll weevil and other pests and frost, hail, rust, smut,

and blight destroying our crops? The answer is we are
drifting away from God. A church in the South
devoted 500 acres to cotton and prayed God to protect
it. While fields all around were devastated by the boll
weevil, not a stem of the church field was injured. Let
Congress appoint a commission (not of politicians but
men who know God and the Bible) to lead the nation
back to the divine law and the divine authority; then
the agricultural question shall be settled, for the earth
shall yield her productions in overwhelming abundance
to a God fearing and law abiding people.

GEO. MCGINNIS

10

Resolutions adopted by the Antioch Baptist Association,
a sodality of colored divines in Chicago:

WHEREAS, Some of our own Countrymen have
their psychology twisted and think by some means that
they are better than the Negro. And,

WHEREAS, it is not the Negro's choice to be thus
discriminated against, dividing and bringing woeful
vengeance upon our great Nation, notwithstanding it is
being done And,

WHEREAS, The race hasn't wealth and other
necessaries to fight its battles, but have souls like anybody else. Therefore, be it

RESOLVED, That we cry unto God out of the depth
of our souls, send up many fervent prayers. Put it
squarely up to God, that He act in keeping with His
word and smash into oblivion, the folly of racial hatred,
discrimination and oppression. The time has fully
ripened that this kind of non-sense must be wiped out
of existence. God would frown upon us and disdain us
as Children of His Handiwork, if we fail to resent such

black insults; and persistently cry unto Him for deliverance from such preposterous evil. Be it further,
RESOLVED, That the Negro Pray as never before. Overwhelm the Throne of our God with soulful prayers. Block up every passage in Heaven. Put on a Blockade in Shechinah land with your prayers, that the Angelics can't egress nor ingress until God looks down with an eye of justice and break in pieces and cast into an ever-lasting abolishment this malignant racial prejudice, even though it cost a more supreme sacrifice than has ever been made in defense of human rights.

II

The gaudy life of a Chicago banker in the Coolidge Golden Age, as reported in a circular describing the new directors' room of the Illinois Merchants Trust Company:

The damask hangings are of two sorts, the narrow panels have stripes of gold upon every seam and the wide panels have no gold on center seam. The narrow panels are from a Roman Palace of the Seventeenth Century. The wide panels are also Roman and contain the coat of arms of the Chigi family. . . . The coat of arms consists of three hills surmounted by an eight pointed star. . . . The table on the left is Roman of the Sixteenth Century. . . . It is a very magnificent Renaissance. On the table is an interesting clock of the French Empire and also two gilded miniatures of the famous columns of Trajan and Marcus Aurelius, in Rome. The directors' table has an inlaid design of the same pattern as that in the rug, both of which were made especially for this room.

12

Progress of Law Enforcement in Chicago, as reported by the distinguished *American*:

A fifteen-year-old boy was shot and killed by a traffic officer in an alley near Wabash avenue and Harrison street today. The boy was shooting craps with playmates and the officer sought to arrest him. He ran and the officer fired, killing him.

13

From the programme of an organ recital at the University of Illinois:

Marche Slave means Slavic or Slavonic march, and not the march of the slaves, as people sometimes guess from the title. Slavic is a general term for the Russians, Poles, Serbs, and kindred races.

14

From an editorial in the *Kiwanis Magazine* by the Hon. Roe Fulkerson:

Kiwanis is no longer a child. Kiwanis is full grown and a club of consequence and standing in every community. This standing and social prominence it gives to these wonderful wives and daughters of ours throw on us a responsibility to live up to them—*LOOK* like what we are.

If this means anything it means an end of affairs in Kiwanis which are marked " Informal." It means that our club, our women folks, our standing, are all as good as any set of men ever had and if so, we must live up to them.

Appearances count. Evening clothes count. Our ladies, our social standing and our organization are entitled to evening clothes.

15

From an article by the Hon. Stewart C. McFarland in the *Rotarian*:

Had an Optimist, Coöperative, Exchange, Lions, Kiwanis or a Rotary Club flourished in the days of the Exodus with old Moses as president, the children of Israel would have reached the promised land in forty days instead of forty years. Would not any of these clubs in the days of Sodom and Gomorrah have saved those cities?

From a laudatory article on the learned justices of the Supreme Court of Illinois in the *Illinois Publisher*:

Mr. Justice Stones . . . is a member of a number of fraternal orders, being a Knight Templar and a member of the Knights of Pythias. He is also a member of the Peoria Rotary Club.

Mr. Justice Thompson . . . is an Elk, an Odd Fellow, a Knight of Pythias, a Moose, an Eagle, a Modern Woodman and a Mystic Worker.

Mr. Justice Heard . . . is a 33rd degree Mason, a member of the Presbyterian Church, an Odd Fellow, a member of the Freeport and Dixon Country Clubs, and a Kiwanian.

INDIANA

1

The rewards of a statesman in the Knobs region of Southern Indiana, as reported by the Evansville *Courier*:

> Uncle Harve Garrison, father of Charles Garrison, Democratic county chairman of Warrick county, presented Senator William B. Carleton, editor of the Boonville *Enquirer*, with two sweet potatoes weighing 11½ pounds, today. Uncle Harve presented these to the senator as a token of his sterling democracy.

2

Modern methods of propagating Christianity in rural Indiana, as described in a Y.M.C.A. press-sheet:

> EVANSVILLE.—When the six-shooter in the hands of Boss Carr sent forth its first roar in the lobby of the Association building Monday night, all the straw bosses and hands jumped about four feet from the floor, and realized that the Y round-up was really on. Decked out in real cowboy togs—broad rimmed hat, red shirt, fur leggins, clanking spurs and a belt full of deadly guns— Boss Carr led the way to chow. "Take off these table cloths," said he to the ladies, "Cowboys can't eat on table cloths; give us the boards after tonight. We're going to treat 'em rough in this campaign." No gentle tapping of the gravel, but the roar of an army pistol

72

which lifted everybody out of their chairs, was the way
in which Boss Carr tried to quell a commotion in the
hall but when one of the husky hands appeared with a
young non-member properly lassoed and tied, and put
on him the Y brand of membership right in front of
the gang the Boss seemed pleased and told the bunch:
" That's the way to get 'em! Don't ask them if they
want to join! Just go get 'em! "

3

From a code of ethics for the clients of barber-shops,
published by the *Journeyman Barber* of Indianapolis:

Don't fold your arms when you lay down in the chair.
It makes a hump on your chest that interferes with the
barber.

Don't chew tobacco or gum while getting shaved.
It's hard enough to shave some men at any time, but it
is almost impossible to properly shave a man whose
jaws are working.

After the barber has given you a good, clean shave,
don't lick the corners of your mouth to find out if he
left a few hairs there.

Always see that your face is clean before getting in the
chair for a shave. If your face is black and grimy, ask
the barber for a towel and cake of soap, and wash up as
soon as you enter the shop. The barber is only too glad
to oblige you in this manner, but no barber likes to
shave a dirty face.

4

From a go-getting pamphlet issued by Wabash College, at Crawfordsville:

A Wabash man is one of the best-known authorities on trust estates in the East.

For six years one of the Senators from Colorado was a Wabashian.

The director of the Y.M.C.A. in Manila is a Wabash man.

A Wabash man gave the Turks one of the finest translations of the Gospel.

A Wabash man is a leading editorial writer on the most important newspaper in Indiana.

The president of the Motion Pictures Producers and Distributors of America is a Wabash man.

A Wabash man is forester of the State of Utah.

The best-known golf architect in the Middle West is a Wabash man.

5

Conclusion reached after five years of prayer and cogitation by the eminent South Bend *Tribune:*

The best and easiest solution of the Prohibition problem would be for people to quit drinking.

6

Scientific note on the Mexican from the distinguished *Lake County Times* of Hammond:

As a general rule, he is not one half as bad as exaggerated newspaper reports make him out. He is human like the rest of us, only his customs and ideas are different from ours. Hence it is our mission to educate him in our ways and thoughts.

7

Effects of the Ku Klux campaign of education at North Manchester, on the Eel river, as reported by the Rev. Thomas M. Conroy in the *Ecclesiastical Review*:

> Some wag spread the report a few weeks ago that the Pope was to reside there incognito until his residence in Washington was completed. The details of his coming were added to the story—the Pope would arrive on the evening train. A crowd estimated at fifteen hundred was at the station to witness his entrance.

8

Application of large scale industrial methods to the concerns of the spirit in the sterling town of Andrews:

> Seventeen hours in one continuous church service to read through the New Testament is the record of the members of the Andrews Methodist Church. . . .
>
> While a group of 25 persons were in the church auditorium reading the New Testament, townspeople of Andrews were reading through the entire Old Testament, so that the entire Bible was read through in 17 hours, beginning Thursday morning at 3 o'clock and continuing until 8 o'clock Thursday night. . . .
>
> Mrs. S. S. Beauchamp of Andrews has the honor of having remained for the longest period in the church service, having stayed there for 14 hours and 40 minutes. Mrs. Wischmeier stayed for 14 hours and 30 minutes, and Mr. Wischmeier stayed throughout the entire 17 hours with the exception of a couple of hours when he was called away. . . . In the church service the book was read from the start to the finish, as it is written, with no interruptions.

9

The evolution of the Higher Journalism in Indianapolis, as reported by the distinguished *Star*:

The *Star*, in 1925, will be a better paper. Numerous steps of advancement have been decided upon. The first marked change will be made when the number of comic pages in the *Sunday Star* will be increased from four to eight.

IOWA

Collapse of the work of the Sulgrave Foundation in Iowa, as reported from Sioux City:

> When Lady Eleanor Smith, daughter of Lord Birkenhead, former lord chancellor of England, smoked a cigarette on the campus of Morningside College here last Wednesday, and when Lord Birkenhead himself produced his own bottle of wine at a luncheon at which he was the guest of the Methodist college professors, they started something. Now the members of the Women's Christian Temperance Union of Sioux City want the world to know that they do not approve of the conduct of the distinguished guests. The women declare that in addition to the aforementioned acts, Lord Birkenhead, just before his lecture at Grace Methodist Church, attended a gathering of lawyer acquaintances in the basement of the church, where he opened for them a bottle of " the king's own." Resolutions adopted by the women declare that " the union wishes to go on record as being opposed to the earl's propaganda against the established laws of this country and the lack of propriety of his daughter."

2

Tart political note in the Des Moines *Capital:*

> For more than 20 years Senator La Follette has not made a really patriotic speech. On no Fourth of July

77

has he stood up and said to the young men of Wisconsin that this republic is the greatest country in the world. In view of Senator La Follette's history the *Capital* would like to inquire on what ground he is entitled to receive one vote for the office of President.

3

Formal termination of the war for democracy in Iowa, as reported by a press dispatch from the up-and-coming town of Lisbon:

Approximately 10,000 persons gathered here from eastern Iowa to attend Sauerkraut Day, formerly an annual event, but abandoned during the war. The crowd ate 120 gallons of kraut, 250 pounds of wieners, and 75 pounds of crackers for lunch, and about the same for supper.

4

Rise of the scientific spirit in the great open spaces, as reported by the Waterloo *Evening Courier:*

Mrs. J. A. Smith, of 223 Vine street, who is interested in observing the license plates on cars while out riding, yesterday was able to complete the observation of licenses from every one of the 99 counties in Iowa. She has seen license plates from very many States also.

5

Bitter fruits of the great crusade in rural Iowa, as reported by the eminent *Iowa Legionaire:*

" Pro-Germanism is so strong in our community we can not have a Legion post! " This astounding assertion was made to the editor of the *Iowa Legionaire* by a Legion comrade in this state. We could hardly believe

it; then we got another shock when we received the
same kind of a report from another Iowa community.
We have investigated. Yes, it's true . . .

6

Progress of Service in the Missions Belt, as reported by
the Odebolt *Chronicle*:

Mrs. M. D. Fox will act as hostess for the Home
Missionary Society of the Methodist Episcopal church
tomorrow afternoon. Mrs. L. T. Quirk will present
the topic, " Our Eastern States: a *Foreign* Missionary
Field."

7

Announcement of a popular mortician in the eminent
Waterloo *Courier*:

Ed Kistner is a very kind-hearted man,
To him you can always appeal;
He goes and gets his corpse at very high speed,
Riding in his big automobile.
Should you meet with death some night you feel
And wanted an undertaker
Ed Kistner will be at your home very quick
For he goes in his big automobile.
No matter how dark the night may happen to be
Just telephone Ed Kistner and he will be there,
For he has light on his big automobile.

8

Literary preferences of the *Feinschmecker* at the Iowa
State College, as reported by the college paper:

" Oh, I always read the *American Magazine*, and
then, if I have any time left, the *Literary Digest* or the

Saturday Evening Post or *Collier's*," the average man on
the campus will answer when asked about the magazines
he is especially fond of. The *American* is the only one
read by practically every man and woman at Ames.

9

Moral warning to the patrons of a leading hotel of Sioux
City:

NOTICE

You are respectfully notified and cautioned that the
management is in no manner responsible for the order-
ing or delivery of any intoxicating beverages to any guest
or patron of this hotel.
All red lights lead to fire escapes.

10

Scientific notice in the renowned Odebolt *News:*

Am in a position to treat your pigs for worms, 12c
each. New oil, improved method. Results guaranteed.
G. W. WISEMAN, Odebolt, Ia. Phone 84

11

The perils that beset a wandering minnesinger in the
Booster Belt, as described by the eminent Des Moines
Register:

Edgar Lee Masters left Des Moines for La Crosse,
Wis., without giving the Des Moines Women's Club an
explanation in regard to the statement he made several
days ago about the smoke nuisance in Des Moines.
Mrs. Eugene Cutler, president of the club, searched the
city in vain to locate Mr. Masters and get him to explain
the alleged insult.

12

Soul-searching in the Chautauqua Belt, from the Odebolt *Chronicle:*

The plays and operas have no place in the chautauqua if it shall continue to be good. We know that the people are wild about plays, although we also know of several who had season tickets who staid away because they knew those plays would not be of any moral good to them or otherwise. People do not have to have some one come to town to show them how to shoot, murder, hug or kiss or anything else that comes so natural to man. It is unnecessary, unwholesome and should be condemned by folks who look at things from a standpoint of clean thinking and right living.

13

From a public harangue by one of the *ordentliche Professoren* at the Iowa State College:

Des Moines has the largest per capita ice cream consumption in America.

The second largest gold-fish farm in the world is located within seventy miles of Des Moines.

The best pair of overalls made on the American continent come from Iowa.

There is no group of two and a half million people in the world who worship God as Iowans do.

14

Melancholy reflection of a Spragueville war hero in the eminent Iowa *Legionaire:*

In the recent election, Legionaire Tony Wirtz was defeated in the race for county sheriff, on account of his religious affiliations. Tony served honorably with the A.E.F. during the war, and possessed all the natural qualifications for the office, having served four years as deputy sheriff, while his opponent never saw a day's service during the war. Such events as these cause me to wonder, "Was it in vain?"

15

Contribution to the secret history of the Republic by the Rev. Harry N. Anderson, a favorite ecclesiastic of Des Moines:

Thank God for Calvin Coolidge! Until he came to the presidential chair, Coolidge had never formally joined a church. He was asked, "Do you believe in Jesus?" "I do." "Do you believe in the church?" "I do." "Then why don't you join the church?" "I will, at once." Thank God for Coolidge, who was big enough to set an example for the people who have elected him President!

16

The metaphysical basis of Rotary, as expounded in an address before Waterloo, Iowa, Rotarians by the Hon. Carl Weeks:

Rotary is not the right of a Rotarian; it is the privilege. The world and men are thinking as they never thought before. Men elected as presidents of Rotary are put there to think. Men have sought to define what Rotary is—what is the secret of its hold upon men. I say Rotary is a manifestation of the divine.

KANSAS

I

Effects of the Volstead Act in rural Kansas, as reported by E. W. Howe:

Talk about liquor drinking in the city! You ought to see it in the country! In the old days when a town man was a drunkard they sent him out into the pure, open spaces to reform, but now it's the farmers' sons that are getting to be drunkards and they send them to town to straighten up. You go out to the country sales around Atchison and you see so much bootleg liquor drinking it's disgraceful. I know fellows in Atchison who have as much as two barrels of bootleg in their cellars.

2

Incident of the Higher Learning at the University of Kansas, as described by the distinguished Lawrence *Daily Journal-World*:

The theme of the opera, " The Secret of Suzanne " which is to be presented at Robinson Gymnasium tonight as the opening number of the University concert program, has been found displeasing to a number of Lawrence citizens. A short sketch of the play, printed last night in the *Journal-World*, told of efforts of Suzanne, a bride, to keep from her husband the knowledge that she was addicted to the use of cigarettes and

83

of the arousing of his suspicion that she was unfaithful when he detects the odor of tobacco smoke in his home. Eventually he discovers her secret and in his relief to find that she is still true to him overlooks her use of tobacco. W. A. McKeever, author of the Kansas anti-cigarette law, read the synopsis of the opera with indignation last night and hastened to call upon University officials to inform them that because of the theme of the opera it was not a proper production to be given under the auspices of the University, where the insidious propaganda doubtless fostered by large tobacco interests might pervert the young students of the University. Mr. McKeever said today that a number of Lawrence people were alarmed over the opera. He placed the blame for the production of the opera on tobacco manufacturing interests of the country.

3

Another from the advertising columns of the same great newspaper:

KKK

The Kansas University Fiery Cross Club extends a cordial invitation to all Klansmen who are students, faculty members or University employees to become affiliated with this club. Address communications to Box 7, Lawrence, Kan., or call at the Klan Headquarters downtown.

4

The motives of a statesman in the Epworth League Belt, as described by the Hon. Carl D. Kelly, of Lawrence:

I have often been asked why I aspire to this position of honor. It is to bring joy to mother's heart in knowing that the people of this District in which her boy resides have confidence in his integrity and feel that he will merit the confidence reposed in him to serve them to the best of his ability in the State Senate. The anticipation of pride when I tell my own boys, after they reach an understanding age, that their daddy has served in the State Legislature. Not the least of all, an opportunity to prove to my friends and supporters that a man can serve in this capacity and not yield to any sinister influences that may be brought to bear upon him.

5

Note on the training of a scientist from the Topeka *Capital*:

Dr. M. F. Perkins, chiropractor, is now located in rooms 207-8 in the new Hotel Kansan. Before taking up the practice of chiropractic, Doctor Perkins operated a cleaning and pressing establishment at 727 Kansas avenue.

6

Decay of Christian rectitude in Kansas, as reported by the celebrated Topeka *Capital*:

Nearly every set in Topeka was represented at the dinner-dance, last night, which marked the formal opening of the Hotel Kansan. Vases of yellow and white flowers formed the table decorations for the dinner, which was the last word in culinary achievement, starting, as it did, with caviar and ending with petit fours. A geisha girl in yellow satin pajamas who passed cigars at the end of the dinner and the fact that one of the women diners smoked a cigarette added greatly to the swankiness of the occasion, making the guests feel that, at last, the town had been admitted to the confraternity of big cities.

7

Public bull issued by the Mayor of Pomona, from the
Pomona *Republican*:

WARNING!

Notice is hereby given that the practice of pitching
horse-shoes anywhere near or upon the public streets
and alleys in the city of Pomona, Kansas, on the Sabbath
day must be stopped. Any person violating this order
will be vigorously prosecuted. J. S. LARGENT, *Mayor*.

8

Triumph of chivalry in Kansas by a narrow margin:

After a heated discussion at two meetings of Capitol
Post of the American Legion, at Topeka, over the
endorsement of the plan of the American committee
for relief of German children, the post finally went on
record, by a small majority, as endorsing the movement.
The fight was hot from the start to the finish.

9

Psychic effects of Prohibition in Kansas, as reported to
the pious Philadelphia *Public Ledger* by the Hon. Jay E.
House, a native of the Kansas steppes:

As in New York, Pennsylvania and New Jersey, the
state of Prohibition in Kansas is whatever you want to
believe about it. If one desires to believe that the
prohibitory laws are enforced, he can easily find thousands of excellent citizens who will agree with him. If,
on the other hand, he desires to believe that Prohibition
is not enforced, he can easily purchase the evidence
necessary to sustain his view. He will not, however,

if he lives in Kansas, publicly express such view. He will confine his remarks to the circle of tried and true friends with whom he engages in wassail and song. In Kansas it is not considered good form to say the prohibitory laws are not enforced. Very few have the courage to defy this convention. What is done openly and without apology in New York, New Jersey and Pennsylvania is done behind the barn or in the friendly obscurity of drawn blinds in Kansas. They're not afraid of the awful liquor they drink out there—if they do drink it—but they're afraid to talk about it. In Kansas if you say drinking is going on you get into trouble. The result is that those who know about it— and a good many do—keep it to themselves.

10

More testimony, this time from the Hon. E. W. Howe:

Near where I live in Kansas, a certain remote county is inhabited mainly by people who are always screaming about the bad habits of the towns and cities. . . . The other day the sheriff of the county made a night raid, and in three towns rounded up twelve distillers of bootleg whisky. All the distillers were farmers. Another bootlegger captured in the same vicinity operated the largest illicit distillery ever found in the United States. The big distiller was a farmer, and for years had been indignant at town people because of their bad habits.

11

Tribute to a worthy lady in the *Federation News*, organ of the State Federation of Women's Clubs:

I wish you could see our new State president preside. When a woman has the floor, whether she excels or whether she blunders, Mrs. Miller's face just beams at her. To the timid one her smile is full of earneft, anxious and affectionate encouragement. To the brilliant one it is full of pride and affection.

If one offers a bright thought she seizes it inftantly and makes much of it. Never tries to take credit to herself, or plumes herself on anything. Juft works and smiles.

12

Lateft triumph of the Higher Patriotism in Kansas, as reported by E. W. Howe:

The attorney general of Kansas has ruled that if a child in school refuses to repeat the flag pledge, its parents may be arrefted and fined. A good many children are tired of repeating the flag pledge every day, which is as follows: " I pledge allegiance to my flag and to the republic for which it ftands, one nation indivisible, with liberty and juftice for all." . . . The pledge was invented, and forced on the children, by an old maid engaged in welfare work.

13

Revolutionary remark credited in the public prints to the Hon. Charles Mann, an eminent Kansas editor:

I am in favor of a law compelling women found guilty of murdering their husbands to make public apology.

14

Law Enforcement report by the Rev. J. David Arnold, of Manhattan:

A terrible condition exifts here. Liquor is apparently flowing freely.

KENTUCKY

Announcement of a candidate for the judicial ermine in the eminent Mt. Vernon *Signal:*

A CARD TO THE VOTERS OF ROCKCASTLE COUNTY:

I am a candidate for County Judge.

The first reason I want to be elected judge is to fill the vacancy occurred by electing S. F. Bowman in 1921.

The second reason is to relieve Mr. Bowman of the great burden placed on him by the sheriff laying down on his job, thereby causing Mr. Bowman to try to fill two official positions.

The third reason I want to be judge is because the county needs a judge.

The fourth reason is I want the salary.

Yours for a square deal to the great common people,—

LEE WARD

2

The service of God in Owensboro, as reported by the eminent *Messenger:*

" Solomon, a Six Cylinder Sport." Could you handle as many wives and concubines as this " Old Bird "? Rev. B. G. Hodge will preach on this subject Sunday night at Settle Memorial. You are welcome.

3

Discouraging report for the year 1924 of the Gospel Home Mission Work, Inc., of Louisville:

MEETINGS

Indoor adult attendance 124,255
Street attendance 33,350
Indoor children attendance 1,929
Prison-jail attendance 2,559
Conversions 560

WORK DONE IN MOUNTAINS OF KENTUCKY

Meeting attendance 63,240
Conversions 86

4

The Higher Learning in the Blue Grass, as described in a current press dispatch:

A course in cross-word puzzles has been added to the curriculum at the college of engineering, University of Kentucky, it was announced Sunday by Dean F. Paul Anderson. Dean Anderson believes cross-word puzzles are educational, scientific, instructive and mentally stimulative, as well as entertaining. His senior students, therefore, will hereafter spend part of their study periods in attempting to solve the squares.

5

Exultant gloat of the boosters of Louisville:

If eight men started from their respective homes in New Orleans, Dallas, Omaha, Minneapolis, Toronto, New York City, Charleston and Jacksonville, and traveled by the shortest and quickest routes until they met, they would shake hands sixteen and one-half yards north of the Customs House on Fourth street, Louisville, on a sewer cap midway between a trolley-pole and a fire plug.

6

Final triumph of the Anti-Saloon League over the Watterson tradition, as reported by the mortal remains of the *Courier-Journal*:

> *Resolved*, that any man who obtains by purchase or otherwise intoxicating liquors or narcotic drugs from an illegal vendor of the same or in violation of the laws of the United States, is hereby declared to be ineligible to be received into a Masonic Lodge under the jurisdiction of the grand lodge of Kentucky, and any Kentucky lodge knowingly electing such a person shall forfeit its charter.

7

Handbill circulated in the rising metropolis of Mt. Sterling by a citizen sworn to Service:

! SENSATIONAL !

Judge Prewitt is Thoroughly Aroused Over the Way Things Are Drifting in Our Community.

Bootlegging rampant in county and city, houses of ill-fame spreading over the city, and the city officials winking at it, nothing doing to prevent it. Mayor and police lay around, play cards and won't volunteer as sworn officers to do their duty, neither will they when warrants are placed in their hands. Our Mayor goes merrily on building a house day by day without a permit; our laws are made a farce of. Directly after our Circuit Judge went on the bench he discovered Paris Green in his pasture and cow lot. You will remember he called a Law and Order Meeting to protect his stock and other's stock. I, W. W. Wilson, and quite a number of others put up checks to the amount of $100.00 each if necessary to ferret out this damnable outrage. Now, fellow-citizens, you are called to do something against known parties in our midst who are not poisoning our stock but our children. Our fathers and mothers, all citizens who love their homes and family will come out tomorrow and hear Judge Prewitt on this, the most damnable curse our city is afflicted with, as the examination of our boys showed in our late war. In the name of God and humanity come out and help save your home and family.

W. W. WILSON.

8

Solemn warning by the Rev. Clarence Walker, pastor of Ashland Avenue Baptist Church, Lexington:

It looks to me like Sunday visiting is one of the biggest enemies we have to contend with at Ashland Avenue Church. It is a sight on Sunday morning to see the cars headed out different pikes filled with whole families. And the fathers and mothers doing this thing are certainly leading their children into hell—yes, I said it, and I'll say it again. Parents who do not take their children to God's house and keep His day holy are leading their children into hell-fire.

9

Heroic words of the Hon. Augustus Owsley Stanley, A. B., as reported by the Lexington *Leader:*

If Governor Fields is right, I am going to stand by him because he is right. If he is wrong, I am going to stand by him because he is a Democrat.

10

Resolution adopted by the board of trustees of the Baptist
Woman's Missionary Union Training School at Louisville:

> Resolved, that in the future no student wearing
> bobbed hair will be admitted, and that those in the school
> now wearing such hair be requested to allow it to grow
> and to wear nets until it has attained proper length.

11

Collapse of the Law Enforcement crusade in rural Kentucky, as revealed by a letter to the editor of the Louisville *Courier-Journal:*

> Some time ago I obtained reliable information con-
> cerning the prevention of conception. I have already
> given this information to a number of girls and young
> women. I shall continue to disseminate this knowledge,
> and I dare anyone, either man or woman, to try to stop
> me.
>
> Mrs. Baker.
>
> Hodgenville, Ky.

12

The American language as she is taught in Kentucky,
from a state paper in the esteemed Anderson *News:*

NOTICE TO TEACHERS!!

> All teachers seem to have the wrong conception of the
> course of study about teaching the grades. I say to all
> teachers that " All grades are to be taught every year.
> Do not quibble about this with your patrons. It must
> be as I say.
>
> The Odd Grades as Major Grades and Even Grades

93

as Minor Grades to be taught in the Even Years. And
the Even grades as Major Grades and the Odd Grades
as Minor Grades in the Odd years. Respectfully,

T. J. LEATHERS, SUPT.

13

Literary news from the Louisville *Courier-Journal:*

" I think, with all my optimism, that there is a falling
away from the higher standards of forty years ago," said
Edwin Markham, author of " The Man With the Hoe "
last night, talking about young people. " One cause
of the lowering of standards has been the reading of
such men as Frederick Nietzche (*sic*) and Walt Whitman." The white-haired, white-bearded poet made
these observations in his room at the Brown Hotel
last night while changing his shirt.... He was getting
ready to appear before the Methodist Students' Conference at Trinity Methodist Church.

14

Evidence of a renaissance of Christianity in the blue
grass, taken from a press dispatch from Frankfort:

Representative Lee Simons, of Louisville, has introduced into the Legislature a bill providing for the
suspension of the State Volstead Act during Home-
Coming Week, and for the planting of mint-beds. The
measure also provides for a special admission-free race
meeting at Churchill Downs, and for the refunding of
all losing wagers made by home-coming Kentuckians.
The bill stipulates that any Prohibition officer who
interferes with any home-coming Kentuckian shall be
forever prohibited from sampling any liquor he may
confiscate.

15

Specimen of modern political prose from an Open Letter addressed by one Kentucky candidate for Congress to another:

Permit me to ask you a few questions. Is it not true that you once had to flee to prevent being mobbed on account of your extreme cruelty to your good wife? Is it not true that an attorney once gave your wife money to buy food for boarders, while you were lying in a drunken stupor in a notorious bootleg dive or saloon? Is it not true that friends of your wife had to rush her out of the city to prevent your killing her? Is it not true that you have been a sot drunkard all your life?

You are the embodiment of all that is coarse, vulgar and revolting. You are a type of man who will set down to a table as a guest and in the presence of your hostess use the most vile and profane language. You are the man who has drawn thousands of dollars from the United States Treasury for time spent in drunken debauchery. You are the man whom politicians would keep in office until you die in order that they may get a few more of the unearned dollars you draw from the Government. You are the man who has earned the sobriquet of " slop jar " in Washington City, where you sit in a drunken stupor nine tenths of your time, while your very competent secretary does all your work, for which you get credit.

LOUISIANA

Progress of Methodist *Kultur* in the home of the Creoles, as reported by a press dispatch from New Orleans:

The old Absinthe House, one of the landmarks in the old French quarter of New Orleans, where, according to repute, Jean Lafitte planned his piratical forays and boasted of what he and Napoleon Bonaparte would do to Messieures les Anglais, was badly damaged last night. Prohibition agents did it all for one quarter of an ounce of absinthe, according to their official report, filed today. In the old courtyard, a door, priceless relic of the old hotel, was smashed. The book in which artists, statesmen, writers and lesser or greater notables had signed their autographs was cast carelessly upon the wreckage littered floor. Because a few drops of absinthe was found in the place, charges of possession and sale of intoxicants were placed against the proprietor.

2

Initial effects of the Higher Learning at the University of Louisiana, as reported by the public prints of New Orleans:

State University freshmen whose heads were shaved last night by upper classmen invaded the Baton Rouge High School today and cut the hair of three teachers and a number of girl students. The teachers who lost their locks were the Misses Ruth Gladney, Cora Dros and Violet Keller. An attempt was made to cut the hair of Mrs. B. W. Pegues and Mrs. Charles Kean, two other instructors, but both resisted strenuously. The freshmen invaded the school during school hours and the boys and girls were dragged into the halls and into the schoolyard, many of the feminine victims in tears. No arrests were made.

3

Cultural item from the estimable Shreveport *Journal:*

A bid of $1,000 has been received by Dr. M. E. Dodd, chairman of the general committee of the Billy Sunday campaign, for the chair used by Dr. Sunday during his evangelistic meetings in Shreveport. This chair will go to the highest bidder.

4

Development and improvement of trial by jury among the Nordic blonds of Tallulah, in the Ku Klux and total immersion belt:

Because a juryman failed to agree to a verdict of guilty in the case of Alvin Calhoun, a Negro accused of murder, a mob took the juror from the jury-room, whipped him, and dipped him in a mud-hole. After his chastisement he returned to the jury-room and agreed to a verdict of murder in the first degree.

5

How Christianity is being spread among the female students of Tulane University, as revealed by a large and highly decorated poster on the bulletin board of the girls' branch of this great institution of learning:

IS CHRIST CAMPUS COMMANDER AT YOUR SCHOOL?
Would you pray to God for a Football Victory? Right?
Are there any unsaved on your campus? Students? Faculty? Servants?
How many unsaved people in walking distance of your campus?
Do students respect the faculty? Raise hats?
Is there a daily prayer-meeting on your campus? Do you go? Who does? Will you start one? Volunteer!
What per cent of your students read the Bible daily? You?
How many minutes a day do you pray? Ever pray thirty minutes by watch? Honest!
In how many rooms on your campus is there a deck of spot cards? A Bible?
How about smoking, cursing, drinking?
What per cent of your students go to Sunday-school? Preaching? Once a day? Twice? Prayer-meeting at a church? Contribute to the church? Belong to the church at school? Study the Sunday-school lesson? . . .
How many fellow students bet on the games? Is this Christian? . . .
How many of your students dance? Is this spiritual?
How many students drink? Gamble? Cheat on exams? Is that theft?
Will a real Christian steal?
How could you be " reckless for Christ "? Ever?

How long since you led a soul to Christ? When
try?...
What per cent of your students will lead prayer? A
jail service; are willing to preach; to be a missionary?
How different would it make your campus to have a
full time religious secretary? Isn't it possible? How?...

6

From a public bull by the Rev. J. B. Culpepper, an
eminent Methodist divine of Haynesville:

Every man ought to marry at the age of 21. I would
put 22 as the limit of singleness for a man. At 23 he
ought to be fined $100 for being a bachelor. The
fine should be raised accordingly every year he remains
single. At the age of 30 he ought to be sent to the
penitentiary for life for the crime of remaining un-
married.

7

Reassuring news from New Orleans in the enterprising
Boston *Telegram*:

Bourbon is the only scarce thing in the way of liquor
here.

8

Workings of the new code of journalistic ethics in New
Orleans, as described in a current dispatch from that
great city:

Horse racing seems doomed in New Orleans and
Louisiana. Newspapers, members of the State Senate
and House of Representatives, politicians and many
influential citizens will ask the next Legislature to kill
the sport of kings here. All because the Business Men's

Racing Association, which is conducting the forty-seven-day race meeting at the fair grounds, sent each of the three newspapers but three free passes made out in the name of the owner, managing editor and city editor and none for the working crew. They also cut out all members of the State Senate and House, discontinued all free badges for women and other citizens who used to get guest badges. In fact the action of the fair grounds management since E. R. Bradley and E. G. Schlieder took charge is such that they have been condemned on all sides and sporting editors of different newspapers here are paying their way into the track to write the results of the races. Consequently they are not passing up flagrant violations of race rules and the like. The stewards were condemned for disqualifying Son o' Unc, a favorite, and one paper said the horse was disqualified to aid the bookmakers. They have been panned and roasted for charging admission to the paddock. Every little fault has been brought to light and this has fired the ministers to action. Newspaper editors who have supported the sport say that they have withdrawn their support and will aid any bill that will kill the races.

MAINE

I

Specimen of laudatory verse by the Hon. Bert M. Fernald, senior United States Senator from Maine:

TO TY COBB

From the warm and sunny southland,
From old Georgia's balmy air,
Comes an athlete strong and sturdy—
On the field none can compare.

Fleet of foot and strong of sinew,
Courage of an order high,
He was christened Cobb (the Tyrus),
But his friends all call him " Ty."

As an all-'round sport and athlete
None can equal or compare;
Plays the game with skill and vigor,
And is always on the square.

Twenty years he has been with us,
Favorite captain of the van,
Always courteous, kind and friendly,
Every whit a gentleman.

Here is hoping for the future—
That for twenty years to come
" Ty " will lead the Tigers onward
And will bring the pennant home.

2

Effects of Prohibition in Maine, which has been dry since 1851, as reported by the distinguished Portland *Advertiser*:

The grand jury for the present term of the Superior Court will have to consider something like 50 complaints that have been made of persons found driving automobiles while under the influence of intoxicating liquors.

3

Gloss upon the foregoing by the *Press-Herald* of the same great city:

When the Eighteenth Amendment was adopted and the Volstead Act was passed, most people who believed in Prohibition thought that the question was settled so far as Maine was concerned. They were mistaken about it. The Eighteenth Amendment made it more difficult for the officers of the law to enforce Prohibition in Maine than it ever was before. There was a good reason for this. The Volstead Act sent up the price of liquor and put ten men into the business of liquor-selling where there was one before. It made bootlegging so profitable that a class of men who would never have become liquor sellers, under the conditions which previously prevailed, entered the business.

4

Dispatch from Orono, seat of the University of Maine, in recent public prints:

If Henry James, society novelist and short story writer of the late Nineteenth Century, were to reappear today one-fifth of the University of Maine freshmen class would expect him to be arrayed as a two gun bandit, according to the results of a questionnaire made known today. Martin Luther was the son of Moses; the author of " Vanity Fair " was William Shakespeare; Disraeli was a poet; and Moses was a Roman ruler, according to some of the other answers submitted in reply to questions. Three hundred and fifty students took the tests.

5

Progress of therapeutic science, as reported by the Kennebec *Journal*, the leading public print of those parts:

S. J. Pole, who is a Naturopath at 185A Main St., Waterville, who came here 3 months ago, is making a remarkable success. The sick people from different States are already flocking to his office from the following States: New York, Mass., and N. H., and a radius of 500 miles. They come on trains, automobiles, horses, donkeys, baby carriages and in every mode of transportation. Of course there has been nobody come in a flying machine yet because S. J. Pole has not provided any air drome on his roof; he is making preparations for out of town people to land on the roof. He is planning to build an air drome for people from a long distance like Cal. Time will tell what he will do. So far he has done wonders in curing people.

6

How the divine blessing has rewarded the labors of a go-getting pastor in Saco, as reported in a current press dispatch:

Mr. Walker . . . pastor of the First Congregational Church, prints his church calendar in all the colors of the rainbow, and sends them every week to more than

2,000 people. He plasters the countryside with his slogans. Newspapers carry big display ads. Spotlights play on the church steeple. Soft, yellow light floods the pulpit at sermon time, the rest of the church being dark. Every night in the week in the parish house there are dancing, radio programs, pool, cards and meetings of all kinds. The young people fairly swarm there. Two years ago the average attendance was fifty. Today it exceeds 1,000.

7

Contribution to historical science by the preëminent Portland *Press-Herald:*

An implicit trust in God and its fulfilment rank among the many recorded facts of history.

8

Moral progress reported by a press dispatch from Waterville:

Women students at Colby College who smoke will be expelled immediately from the institution, it was announced by Miss Nettie N. M. Runnels, Dean of the Woman's Division, in letters sent last night to the parents of all girls enrolled in the school.

9

Proud record of an eminent sign and carriage painter of the rising town of Bath, as reported by the correspondent of the Portland *Press-Herald:*

Since film productions were introduced in Bath, away back in 1907, Mr. William K. Hall has missed but six performances in all of the theatres, and has a 100%

record so far as the Opera House, which opened in 1913, is concerned. During Bath's exceptionally prosperous days . . . there were three theatres in the city, and Mr. Hall usually attended three shows a day.

10

Qualifications of a lecturer on economics, as reported by the learned Bangor *Commercial:*

Dr. G. W. Dyer . . . will lecture at the Bangor Chamber of Commerce. . . . The National Association of Manufacturers has secured his services for a year, during which time he will cover the entire country in an effort to give correct information on all economic matters. . . . He is one of the strongest advocates in the country of the principle of the open shop. He is strictly American and a great home-lover, believing in the individual home and large families. He also believes in schools. . . .

MARYLAND

1

Effects of the soft Southern air upon the pronunciation of words in *-orn*, as revealed by an elegiac stanza in the eminent Baltimore *Afro-American:*

> He shall sleep, but not forever,
> There will be a glorious dawn;
> We will meet to part, no never,
> On that Resurrection Morn!

2

Medical miracle in the shadow of the Johns Hopkins Medical School, described by Uncle Jim Keeler, of 3706 Thirty-second Street, Mt. Rainier:

My stomach was in such a bad fix for fourteen years that I couldn't eat anything fried, or fatty, not even butter. In fact, I could eat scarcely anything and my stomach would puff and swell to twice its normal size. I would have terrible pains in the stomach and back and also frightful dizzy spells. The truth is, my condition was so deplorable for those fourteen years that I was unable to work at all. Finally I was attracted to Tanlac, by a testimonial of an old G. A. R. comrade of mine, who testified that he felt twenty years younger after taking Tanlac. I knew him to be a truthful man, so I lost no time in getting some Tanlac. After finishing the first bottle I noticed the puffing and swelling was not

so bad. So I kept taking Tanlac for about five months
and all my distress and pains left me. I now eat and
digest everything and they can't get the food too fat
for me. I am now eighty years old.

3

Note on the functions of a public library, from the annual
report of the Enoch Pratt Free Library of Baltimore:

Since the library is the only institution supported by
the municipality for the inspiration of the citizens, this
high privilege has been accepted as laying upon us the
corresponding duty of placing within reach of all such
books as will give readers . . . a higher sense of the
reality and importance of the future life. . . .

4

From an official report on the industrial situation in Balti-
more by the Hon. Thomas Nolan, vice-president of the
International Brotherhood of Boilermakers, Iron Ship
Builders and Helpers of America:

The crafts on the Western Maryland Railroad done
everything possible to avoid a strike and had representatives on that system for months in an effort to negotiate
a settlement and failed, and the crafts on that system of
railroad realizing the rank injustice that had been done
them, was compelled to come out on strike to protect
their agreement and welfare in the future, came out on
strike March, 1922, and are still out—until that
industrial kaiser in Baltimore realizes that he is dealing
with real men who know what they came out on strike
for, and fully intend to remain on strike until victory
crowns their efforts, let it be sooner or later, and in

connection with that strike I desire to say that the members of Lodge 578 of the International Brotherhood are a bunch of stickers for what is right and honorable and doing everything possible to make the strike effective and successful, never was looking for trouble, but did everything in their power to prevent trouble on many occasions, and where honest business was at stake—they never was found wanting in joining the majority or coming to the rescue at all times when necessary, and did so in March, 1922, and are still there and will remain there until justice takes her proper place when injustice is dethroned and real union men are recognized as one of the principal factors in operating a railroad as it should be, SUCCESSFULLY.

5

Rise of the scientific spirit among the amphibious Fundamentalists, as shown by an advertisement of University Baptist Church in the Baltimore *Sunpaper:*

Dr. Melvin G. Kyle, one of the world's greatest archaeologists, will conduct a School of Biblical Research in this church this week. Dr. Kyle has just returned from explorations in Palestine. His purpose was to dredge the Dead Sea in search of the ruins of Sodom and Gomorrah.

6

Specimen of elegiac verse from the obituary columns of the eminent Baltimore *Sunpaper:*

Two years have passed, our heart's still sore,
As time goes on we miss you more.
Both sad and sudden was his call,
His sudden death surprised us all.

7

Pious note from the estimable *Manufacturers Record* of Baltimore, the organ of the Christian cotton-mill owners of the Confederacy:

Charles E. Waddell, an engineer of Asheville, N. C., in a recent conversation with an officer of *The Manufacturers Record* stated that after reading the paper in his office he took it to his home, where his children eagerly read it, and when they had finished with it he sent it to his daughter, who is studying at Bryn Mawr College, and she, he reported, is intensely interested and gets a great deal of valuable information from every issue. . . .

Some time ago a Baltimore woman of German birth, but a devoted Christian, recalled from a prominent Eastern college her daughter, even when she was in the graduating year, stating that she found that the atheistic German teachings in that college were of such a character that she was afraid if her daughter remained there she would lose her soul, and she would rather that she lose her education than her soul. How many other parents are watching the situation as carefully as she was doing and thus in time learning to act before atheistic teachings have destroyed the religious beliefs of their children? And how many, like Mr. Waddell, are taking care to see that publications pointing out the evils of socialism and communism are sent to their boys and girls who are away from home or furnished to those at home?

8

Progress of the campaign for Law Enforcement in the Methodist slums of the Maryland Free State, as revealed by a letter from Elkton to the illustrious Baltimore *Sunpaper*:

> Cecil county has more Ku Klux in it than any county in the State. She has also more moonshiners, more bootleggers and gamblers than any other, even than Baltimore city. I heard a constable say that to his own personal knowledge there are over 100 men in the business, with at least 50 stills in operation; yet it is one of the main strongholds of law enforcement. Things are so bad in Cecil that at the last term of court Judge Adkins asked for the aid of the people to enforce the law. Yet many cases are known where the strongest kind of evidence was rejected by the jury.

9

New zoölogical classification from the estimable Baltimore *Evening Sun*:

> Two men were sentenced to jail for 30 days and a negro for six months in the Traffic Court today.

10

Aesthetic note from the *Sunpaper*:

> Perhaps the best answer to the question of why a jazz band should be spoken of as a serious musical enterprise is found in the box-office receipts.

11

Strange nocturnal diversion of a Johns Hopkins scientist, as reported by the *Evening Sunpaper*:

> Dr. Robert W. Wood, professor of experimental physics, has been studying for 20 years, with marked success, the fundamental nature of night.

12

New sure cure perfected by Prof. Dr. J. F. Dirzuweit, inventor of the New Life System, with headquarters at Baltimore:

Lying on the couch or sinking down in your easy chair, make sure that every muscle is relaxed. *First, deliberately make your right leg heavy, then the left.* Think of each joint—ankle, knee, hip—to make sure that no muscle is holding any of these parts tense. Relax the trunk; make sure that no single muscle of your back is supporting you in any way. Be sure also to relax the muscles of the face and neck. The jaw must not be clenched; the tongue must not press forward against the teeth nor back against the palate. Now close your eyes. Roll them slightly upward, fixing them on a point far off, on an imaginary horizon. Now gather in your wandering thoughts and try to fix your mind upon a pleasant *blue color.* Visualize, with your eyes closed, a deep blue sky, endless as to dimension. This will aid you to relax, and you will probably feel the desire to go to sleep. Breathe deeply about twenty to thirty times. After this rest, you may return to work. You will find that you have recharged your nervous system with vital force and that you have gained strength and poise for the rest of the day.

13

Lingering effects of the late war for democracy upon jurisprudence in the Maryland Free State, as revealed by an advertisement in the *Sunpaper:*

LAWYER WANTED
To Enter Suit Against a
PRO-GERMAN CONCERN
Address Purchasing Agent, 5870, Sun.

III

14

Mortuary dithyrambs by the Hon. Walter G. Slappey, of 12 Boyd Avenue, Takoma Park, Md., as embalmed in print by the estimable Takoma *News:*

> Woodrow Wilson is gone, gone; but his spirit goes
> marching on! on!!
> For freedom of thought, word and speech, ho! ho!!
> That was our grand President, Woodrow.
> Woodrow Wilson is gone, gone; but his spirit goes
> marching on! on!!
>
> Even yet his noble plans will prevail; and on Earth
> Fatherhood of God and Brotherhood of Man is not
> doomed to fail, ho! ho!!
> That is the spirit of our grand President, Woodrow.
> Woodrow Wilson is gone, gone; but his spirit goes
> marching on! on!!
> His spirit goes marching on!! on!!!

15

From a tract by Dr. Howard A. Kelly, emeritus professor in the Johns Hopkins Medical School:

> I look with equanimity upon evolution, or any other theory, nor do I care (relatively speaking) whether it is true or false, but I do care a great deal to drive men back to God's Word, the fountain of living waters, and *that they shall hold it to be true from Genesis i to Revelation xxii.*

MASSACHUSETTS

I

Questions and answers from examination papers submitted by Boston policemen seeking promotion:

Q. After an accident you find that a machine was being driven by a 15-year-old boy who—lost his life in the collision. A licensed chauffeur was riding with him and was uninjured. Of what crime, or crimes, if any, is he guilty?

A. He was illegal to have allowed a dead boy to operate that car.

Q. What is the difference between a felony and a misdemeanor?

A. A felony comes on the little finger and results in death but a misdemeanor affects the neck and is curable.

Q. You discover the body of a well dressed person on your route. What should be your course of action?

A. Watch the body and see that it did not move.

Q. What do you understand by the term habeas corpus?

A. Habeas corpus is a disease from which human beings sometimes become unconscious.

Q. Define homicide.

A. It means death when least expected.

Q. In the course of your tour of duty you come across a man who is bleeding freely from a deep gash in his leg. What would you do?

A. If sober, I would ask him how it happened. If

not, I would call the wagon and have him arrested for obstructing a public highway.

Q. You are called by the conductor of a street car to help eject a drunken man from the car. What should you do?

A. That is up to the conductor unless he has a warrant. I would tell him to eject the drunken man, for he has no right to assault him, but to throw him off the car, and if he falls on my beat I will take some action.

2

Confused but beautiful peroration of an oration by the Hon. Everett W. Hill, first vice-president of International Rotary, before the intelligent Rotarians of Springfield:

Rotarians, trail blazers of honesty and correct business practises, when our tasks of life near completion may we halt a moment at the brink and, turning look backward o'er the span of life, and, when our eyes shall be turned for the last time to behold the sun in the evening, may they not see a land given over to selfishness. Rather, let their last lingering glance behold the flag of Rotary unfurled full high in the heavens, its arms and its trophies streaming with all their original beauty, not a single spoke erased or polluted and not a single cog removed; bearing for its motto no such miserable interrogatory as " How much can I get with the least possible effort? " but the beautiful sentiment everywhere shining in characters of living light emblazoned on all its ample folds as they float over the sea and over the land, and in every wind under the heaven, that motto dear to the heart of every true Rotarian: " Service above self."

3

From the Boston *Traveler's* able report of an exhibition
of funeral furnishings at Horticultural Hall:

It is the theory of the undertakers that the time has
come to approach the matter of funerals with the same
sanity and coolness shown in coping with any other
inevitable situation.

" You make a will. Many persons select their own
burial lots. Why not caskets and other funeral necessi-
ties? " a leading undertaker asked a reporter.

A few visitors proved their presence to be due merely
to a morbid curiosity, but they were soon given to
understand that their presence was not appreciated.
Not one person among the general public, so far as
could be learned, evinced a desire to buy a coffin,
although many sincere queries were made of the sales-
men as to the character of the material and linings of the
elaborately wrought caskets. The latter are not sold
direct to the public, however, but only to undertakers.

The women were interested most in the burial gowns
of vivid hues and fashionable design, which, as a matter
of fact, could not be distinguished by the ordinary
person from afternoon or evening gowns. Three live
models are showing them.

A six-piece orchestra, for which the mezzanine floor
was cleared, played popular airs last night for the entertainment of the general public and visiting undertakers.

A number of children, passing by on their way to and
from nearby schools, insisted on being admitted to the
hall yesterday until told by the door man, " There's
nothing in here but caskets." They turned and fled.
Three old men, all above 70, were sorely disappointed
when they learned they could not be admitted to a
lecture on embalming.

4

The Higher Learning at Smith College, glimpsed in a dispatch to the eminent Springfield *Republican* from Northampton:

A pickled monkey, which once acted in one of D. W. Griffith's pictures, is perhaps the strangest gift ever presented to Smith College, which has received many useful, ornamental and historically valuable presents.

5

From an advertisement of a treatise on literary composition by Prof. Samuel Thurber, of the Newton High School:

These exercises furnish methods for increasing a student's power of mastering thought, and perfecting his skill in making that thought articulate. They include excerpts from the writings of . . . Brander Matthews, Henry van Dyke, and Calvin Coolidge.

6

Proud boast of the *Hampshire Gazette* of Northampton, the seat of Smith College, of the Clarke Institute for Deaf Mutes, and of the State Hospital for the Insane:

Few cities turn upon their neighbors greater floods of polished virginity at commencement time each year than does Northampton.

7

Survival of New England transcendentalism in the columns of the esteemed Lynn *Telegram-News:*

CLAIRVOYANT—Satisfaction guaranteed. I bring back lost articles, sweethearts, husbands, increase salary. Advice on love, marriage, divorce, business; never fail. Got husband for lady who prayed 30 years for one. M. Perry, Perry Bldg., 71 Market St. Tel. 960.

8

The intellectual life of Boston, as described by the estimable *Evening Transcript*, organ of the New England *Kultur*:

The closing feature of the 1924 Grand Lodge reunion of the Benevolent and Protective Order of Elks came this noon when, in front of the Copley-Plaza Hotel, James G. McFarland of Watertown, South Dakota, the retiring Grand Exalted Ruler of the order, was presented with a Marmon touring car. It was the gift of Boston Lodge No. 10, sponsor of the convention. The car is finished in the Elks' colors. The body is purple with white stripings. On each forward door, in gold letters, are the words, " Official Car, Grand Exalted Ruler," while on each rear door is the Grand Lodge insignia, of clock, star, Elk's head and the American flag. The wheels are done in white, the covers of the two spare tires are of white with purple beading and the top cover is similarly finished.

9

From the rules and regulations for the government and use of the Charles River Reservation at Boston:

Rule 4. No person shall solicit the acquaintance of or annoy another person; or utter any profane, threatening, abusive or indecent language or loud outcry; or solicit any subscription or contribution; or have possession of or drink any intoxicating liquor; or play any game of chance; or have possession of any instrument of gambling; or do any obscene or indecent act; or preach; or pray aloud; or make an oration or harangue, or any political or other canvass; or move in a military or civic parade, drill or procession; or lie down upon a bench or go to sleep thereon; or play any musical instrument except by written authority from said Metropolitan Park Commission.

10

From the learned and distinguished Springfield *Republican*:

A firm belief that Calvin Coolidge became President in accordance with a divine plan and that he should be maintained in office in order that the plan may be carried through forms the keynote of Mayor Edwin F. Leonard's campaign. . . . In the mayor's opinion, any attempt to sidetrack Coolidge now would be a deliberate effort to frustrate the plans of Almighty God and would be attended by certain disaster.

11

Specimen of political prose from the Boston *Evening Transcript*:

At the Cleveland convention the Republican party which Abraham Lincoln founded was given a new birth of freedom under Calvin Coolidge, . . . whose spiritual endowment includes a New England conscience, a national vision, fear of God and faith in man.

12

From the eminent Boston *Herald's* advance notice of the Order of New England Workers, a super-Kiwanis lately founded by high-speed, bean-burning go-getters:

Initiation rites include wearing the New England button at all times and familiarity with the greeting,

which, the committee has suggested, be something like
" Hello friend," " Hi, brother," " Howdy, New
Englander," " 'Lo, Ol' Booster " or " any other cheerful, friendly, optimistic salutation." The grip is to be
a " good, hearty, firm New England hand-clasp, neither
too high nor too low, but on a sort of natural, common,
easy level."

13

Gallant effort of the ancient Puritan spirit to protect itself
against the wop invasion, as reported by the Boston *Globe:*

A mother of six children, Mrs. Nunziatine Ventura,
32, of 184 Cottage St., East Boston, was sentenced to a
year in jail today by Judge Charles J. Brown, in the
East Boston District Court. Ludovico d'Appolito, 42,
received a similar sentence in the Deer Island House of
Correction. They were charged with living together as
husband and wife.

14

From a solemn guarantee issued by the late Henry Cabot
Lodge, LL.D., in February, 1921:

Senator Fall is a thoroughly upright and highminded
man, and utterly incapable of using his office for his own
financial interest.

15

From a St. Patrick's Day oration at Boston by the Hon.
W. T. A. Fitzgerald, an eminent historical scholar of
those parts:

The Father of his Country placed unbounded confidence in the patriotism and loyalty of his Irish generals
and soldiers, who compromised *approximately one-half
of the entire Revolutionary Army.*

16

Sweet, lovely writing in an editorial in the Boston *Transcript*:

Dreamy May! Not so much of childhood as of adolescence do you savor. April's laughter and tears have given way to a wistful, listening mood that knows not itself. Powers are under way that can as yet scarce reveal themselves, yet which gently shake the being with the prescient touch of their spirit. Such is youth, leafing youth.

17

The New Thought method of snaring a husband, as described in the *Nautilus Magazine*, of Holyoke:

Make up your mind that God knows the right man, that God *now* brings you and the right man together IN SPIRIT.

Now, the only way that the right man can find you is for you to so express yourself that all men looking upon you may see your good work, your radiant spirit, and may *glorify the loving Father within you.*

In short, begin to *express yourself*, instead of sitting around and praying or affirming or longing to have God hand you this particular man on a silver platter!

18

Biological secret of Dr. Coolidge's immortality, revealed by the alert and learned Lowell *Courier-Citizen*:

President Coolidge, according to an interesting genealogical study, . . . is the second President . . . who is a descendant of Deacon Edmund Rice, of England, who settled . . . in this State in 1636. . . . Among the more famous . . . of the Edmund Rice breed may be mentioned . . . Mary Baker Eddy, founder of Christian Science.

19

Effects of Woman Suffrage as disclosed by the Lynn *Telegram-News*, a great intellectual and moral organ:

Many of the village belles . . . of Danvers . . . have started wearing dog collars. Dog collars are not only being worn by school girls, but are even worn by teachers. . . . The girls do not always buy their dog collars. That fact was brought to light when many complaints were heard from dog owners to the effect that dogs have mysteriously lost their neck pieces.

MICHIGAN

1

Fostering the Higher Learning at the University of Michigan:

The University of Michigan Club of Detroit is responsible for entering about twelve athletes in the University this Fall. This required hard work, as positions had to be secured for the Summer and also for the school year. Michigan was sold to these boys, even though they had received attractive offers from other schools.

2

From a hortatory article in the *Kiwanis Magazine* by the Hon. Verner W. Main, president of the Kiwanis Club of Battle Creek, 1919-1921, and of the Chamber of Commerce, 1922:

The only fair attitude of any member of a community toward his Chamber of Commerce is that of an honest search after, and a willingness to promote, such activities in the Chamber of Commerce as will best serve to make his Chamber of Commerce the kind of Chamber of Commerce he would like.

3

Specimen of philosophical verse by the poet Fred Barron, of Detroit, from the *Shoe Retailer*:

Silent beasts of burden,
Those wondrous man-made shoes,
Unfortunately you were created slaves
To carry us where'er we choose.

Thru the mud, thru the snow,
Thru the streams where waters flow,
And never a whisper of discontent,
Those wondrous shoes on their mission bent.

Protectors of the feet of man,
With great delight in you we stand;
In all our biddings that you must do
Your services are praiseworthy, you wondrous shoes.

4

The qualifications of the jurist in Michigan, as described in a circular received by alumni of the State university:

I am enclosing cards of Guy A. Miller, who is a candidate for the office of Circuit Judge. Back in '96 to '99, Judge Miller was pitcher on one of the best baseball teams Michigan ever had. In 1898 and 1899 he had a record of twenty-seven games won and four lost.

5

State of Christian civilization in Detroit, as described by the Hon. Wayland D. Stearns, a distinguished uplifter of the town:

There are ten times as many murders in Detroit as in

the whole of England. . . . There are over 40,000 women here who are immoral. There are more than 100,000 men who are " cheaters." Venereal disease has gone up to twenty times what it was a few years ago.

6

Rise of ritualism among Michigan Babbitts, as reported by the *American Lumberman:*

At a rousing banquet of Hoo-Hoo held at Grand Rapids laſt week the rafters one moment were ringing with the ſtrains of " Sweet Adeline " and " Lil' Liza Jane," and then—

Some one arose and said simply, " I think we should all ſtand a moment in memory of our former President, Woodrow Wilson." The two hundred or more men present arose as one. Then—a cry, " Face the Flag! " came from the rear of the room. All turned toward the large banner draped behind the speaker's table and, moved by a single impulse, joined in singing the national anthem.

7

The process of Law Enforcement in Detroit, as revealed in the eminent *Times'* report of a case before Simons, J.:

After the jury had been charged, one of its members asked the court whether the word " ſtatute " used throughout the case, meant a human being. The judge explained that the word meant the written law.

8

Editorial pronunciamento of the celebrated Flint *Daily Herald:*

Any man of the Twentieth Century who will . . . ſtand for Evolution is not, despite his appearance from a physical standpoint, a member of the race of human-kind. . . . The very fact that the sun rises in the east EVERY MORNING and sets in the WEST EVERY EVENING, is sufficient proof for MOST OF US that there is a God. Why doesn't it set in the NORTH once in a while for a change? BECAUSE THAT ISN'T GOD'S PLAN.

9

How the study of comparative religions is carried on at the University of Michigan, as described by the *Michigan Daily*, the official students' paper:

> The students will meet for supper and the consideration of Mohammedanism and Buddhism at 6.30 o'clock. Believers in these oriental faiths will speak of them from affectionate knowledge. Maurine Bauer is a whistling artist of great ability and will assist in the program. Laurette Taylor in "Peg o' My Heart," will illustrate the religious service at 7.30 o'clock. Bring nothing less than a dime for the collection.

10

Progress of the new moral legislation in Michigan, as described in a dispatch from Kalamazoo:

> Finding police officials handicapped by the lack of an ordinance giving them regulatory control over ice-cream parlors, City Attorney Marvin Schaberg has drawn up an ordinance providing for the licensing of such places.

11

Specimen of literary criticism by the eminent chief editorial writer of the Detroit *Free Press*:

> The true mission of the novel is to entertain in hours

of weariness or in time of recreation, and when writers try to make it do something else, they become a good deal of a nuisance.

12

The Higher Learning in Kalamazoo, as reported by the world-famous *Gazette:*

The degree of master salesman, the highest award granted to boys who represent the firm, has been awarded to Stanley Stewart, 14, son of William H. Stewart, 711 Denner street, by the Curtis Publishing Company.

13

The worship of Jahveh the Baptist in the same great city:

SUNDAY NIGHT

SURPRISE

Cheerful ushers show you to comfortable seats. Bright illumination greets you. At 7 sharp Mr. Klump leads the RE-JOY-SING of gospel songs—and how everyone does sing! Then comes an inspiring selection by vested

CHORUS CHOIR

In a few moments, toctoc, lights are dimmed and a spot light shines on Dr. G. H. Young, Pastor, who speaks briefly on

" *The Seven Modern Wonders of the World !* "

An evangelistic sermon—absolutely! As the pastor concludes, the pipe organ (played by a talented lad in his teens) is heard and now the rich contralto voice of Loreen Schricker sings to you. Then—lights on! And as you leave the church, the latest copy of a popular 25c magazine is handed you with the compliments of the publishers. Yes, this is free—but aren't life's greatest things; pure air, sunshine, love, laughter and religion all free, too?

GIFT NIGHT TOMORROW
Sunday at 7 : 00
FIRST BAPTIST CHURCH
" IN THE HEART OF THE CITY "

14

Specimen lyrics from a book of instructions to motorists, composed and published by the Detroit *Polizei:*

I

There are drivers that make us happy,
　　There are drivers that make us sad,
There are drivers that take away all pleasure
　　Which from motoring might be had.
There are drivers who always hog the roadway,
　　Give no signals wherever they are,
But the driver that fills my life with sunshine
　　Is the driver who drives with care.

II

You can lead a horse to water
　　But you can't make him drink.
We can give you the thought
　　But we can't make you think.

15

Extract from a public harangue by the Hon. Mr. Evans, Imperial Wizard of the Ku Klux Klan, at Jackson:

We'll take every child in all America and put him in the public schools of America. My son and daughter and all other children will go side by side to school. We will build a homogeneous people; we will grind out Americans just like meat out of a grinder.

MINNESOTA

I

Spread of the ideal of Service to the lumber barons, as revealed by a harangue before the Northwestern Lumbermen's Association at Minneapolis by the Hon. Charles D. Marckres, of Perry, Iowa:

As I sometimes wonder about the problem of life and the reason that we lumbermen are permitted to live and enjoy the blessings of this earth, the thought has occurred to me that we are expected to do something more than accumulate wealth for ourselves or build up large business enterprises, or just have all the fun that we can. I sometimes think that our real purpose is to build and create the desire for building homes. And as my thoughts have rambled along that direction, I have wondered whether, when the time comes that we stand before the Great Judge, we could gain anything more than a judgment that would be pronounced something like this: " Well done, thou good and faithful servant. As you have provided homes on earth for my children, even so have I provided a home here for you where everlasting happiness and eternal peace shall be your reward in Heaven."

2

From the report of a committee of the Hennepin county grand jury, appointed to inspect the city morgue at Minneapolis:

We found in this last station of the dead
One lonely man, spaced in his narrow bed.

We saw his face; his arms, crossed on his breast,
Were folded there for an eternal rest.

Still was the pulse, stopped the fleeting breath,
He lay there wrapped in mystery and majesty of death.

About this place there is no hint of gloom,
Bright sunshine floods the air in every room.

With cheerful mien toward the door we strayed,
Leaving a kindly thought for he that stayed.

May Charon, crossing Styx in leaden boat and oars,
Bear him, with coin in lips, to Lethe's farthest shores.

3

Apothegm by the gifted Francis Burgette Short, A.B., D.D., in the program-book of the twenty-second annual convention of the Northeastern Minnesota Educational Association:

Teachers have no right to think as they please unless they please to think right.

4

Ghoſtly news from the city of St. Paul, reported to the
eſtimable *Atlantic Monthly* by Dr. Glenn Clark, professor
of English at Macaleſter College:

> I wish that I lived nearer Boſton so that I could have
> a little conversation with you and relate some of the
> amazing answers to prayer that have come to me in the
> paſt two years. When I say that I have had one hundred
> answers to prayers in the laſt six months, I am putting
> it very conservatively.

5

The Higher Learning at the University of Minnesota, as
reported by a bulletin of the Trade News Service:

> Work is under way at the University of Minnesota to
> eſtablish definite buying ſtandards by which the public
> may be able to choose and buy clothing wisely, with
> regard to general economy, fit and ſtyle, according to
> Marion Weller, Associate Professor of Textiles and
> Clothing in the Division of Home Economics. In a
> letter to Roy A. Cheney, Executive Secretary of the
> Associated Knit Underwear Manufa〜urers of America,
> at Utica, N.Y., Prof. Weller says in part:
> " Have you any available information which will be
> of help on setting up for the consumer ſtandards by
> which she may be able to choose and buy underwear
> wisely? Will it be possible for you to answer some of
> the queſtions that are conſtantly arising in regard to
> knit underwear? "

6

Christian sport at the University, as reported by the Associated Press:

> Just before the kick-off the players gathered in a group and Clarence Schutte, who turned out to be the star of the game, led his mates in a short prayer.

7

Specimen of news-writing in the Bible Belt, from the Bethel *Banner*:

> The C. M. A. Convention at the Bethel Church was a grand success, and God signified His approval by saving precious souls. Thursday night, Brother Langmade delivered the message and souls wept their way into the kingdom. Friday, Brother E. E. Johnson delivered a stirring message and God again answered by saving souls. Saturday and Sunday Brother Uncle Morgan of Windom delivered the messages and what the fruitage was only eternity will tell.

8

Effects of the Harding literary style upon the native minstrelsy of Minnesota, as revealed by an ode by Miss Marianne Clarke, of St. Cloud:

> Our Constitution is commemorated
>   By Puritan Fathers who arbitrated
> The grand ideals of our glorious past,
>   May they inspire forever and cast
> Abiding faith in our Declaration
>   For United States seek ratification
> Of Law and Order, Progress and Peace—
>   Oh! heroes of old may thy spirit increase.

Our Constitution is the best that we know
" Go To It," stand by it, as they did long ago,
Washington, Madison, Franklin so clever
Fifty-six men were in council together;
John Marshall started the Supreme Court so great
Now is there another Marshall to " fete "
To assemble the group of nineteen twenty-four
A world Court of Justice from shore to shore?

Practical Peace in International Relations
The power of man in Brotherhood of Nations
Strong, Righteous Service to the land of the free
America first for you and for me.
Five Presidents arose and gave us their lives,
Yes, including " Harding," all sacrificed,
The secret of life is " Be Just and Be True—
To Our Constitution—and the Red, White and
Blue."

9

Warning to amorous motorists on a police sign at Lake
Johanna:

Side curtains not permitted unless it is raining.

10

Picture of the Nordic Blond paradise drawn by a con-
tributor to the *Journal* of the American Medical Association:

I have lived in Minnesota, the land of Magnus
Johnson, for thirteen years, a western Scandinavia where
the birds sing in Swedish, the wind sighs its lulabyes in
Norwegian, and the snow and rain beat against the
windows to the tune of a Danish dirge.

MISSISSIPPI

I

Obscene effects of Negrophile infection among the Ku
Kluxers, as reported by the *Tennessee Fiery Cross* of
Memphis:

> It was our privilege to watch one day recently upon
> the streets of Jackson, Miss., the impressive greeting of
> a white professor of Tougalloo University to a Negro
> couple who were evidently upon his calling list. Rushing
> wildly across the street to greet them and removing his
> hat, he grasped them successively by the hand, calling
> them Mr. and Mrs. and assuring them of his delight
> at the meeting, and his desire for further and closer
> association. To the everlasting credit of the Negroes
> let it be stated that the demeanor of the sheep-killing
> dog was a model of heroism compared with the manner
> in which they looked right and the left, and frantically
> departed. Their discomfort eloquently bespoke their
> realization of the impropriety of the entire proceedings
> and was a rebuke of a nature to make the flesh of a
> Southern white man crawl.

2

Tribute to a talented technician from the *Cotton Farmer*
of Scott, Miss.:

> Miss Lizzie Young, the daughter of Mr. Henry
> Young, of Triumph Plantation, was happily married to

Mr. Willie McCalib, on Thursday in Greenville. Willie is the efficient hostler on McConnell Plantation, and has acted in that capacity from the time he was fifteen years old. He has proved a faithful young man in his job and up to the present is always on the job. He claims to have less sick mules than any of the other hostlers on the job, and loses less mules by death, than any of the other hostlers. Really the job of hostler is an important one and every man or boy is not fitted for the job. It takes special qualifications to be a hostler worth while. The waste of mule power in the Cotton Belt is enormous and is a great drain on the resources of the Cotton Belt. A good deal of this waste could be avoided by a little care on the part of the hostler.

3

Effects of war poetry upon the Guntown correspondent of the distinguished Memphis *Commercial Appeal*:

The Baptist ladies of Guntown served a most delightful chicken dinner, and dozens of hens gave their all to satisfy the appetites of the town people.

4

Contribution of the Biloxi Rotarians to Service, as reported in a current news dispatch:

The Biloxi Rotary Club met at the Desporte Packing Company's plant and was served a seafood dinner with Ernest Desporte, Jr., as host. Dr. A. B. Badendreer presented a plan for bringing the various nations of the world together in permanent harmony by the placing of emblems to be known as the Rotary Peace Emblem over the entire universe. The matter will be referred to Rotary International.

5

How the exercises of the intellect are combined with the worship of God in the bottom lands along the Pearl river, as described in a dispatch from Marks to the public gazettes of Jackson:

The regular monthly social meeting of the Layman's League was held at the library last night. The devotional exercises were conducted by the president, E. C. Black, Psalm 119: 67-71-75, and Leviticus XXVI 2-5, were read and afterwards discussed by those present. Prayer by Mrs. G. C. Jones was had. After the devotional exercises it was announced that A. A. Pogue, M. D. Brett, C. W. Carr and E. C. Black had been selected for debate. The former two were given the affirmative side and the two latter, the negative. Their subject, " Resolved, That Andy Gump, Being 100 Per Cent American, Should Be Elected President of the United States."

6

The moral equivalent of mah jong and jazz in Vicksburg:

The Negro was hauled up five feet but slipped back. The sight of the nude body rising above the crowd increased the excitement. " Shoot him! " someone called. " No, no," came the answer, " let him die slow." Seeing that he was merely suffering discomfort, men below began to jerk his legs. Others smeared kerosene upon the body, while others prepared a bonfire below. The Negro assumed an attitude of prayer, raising his hands, palms together. The whole affair was witnessed by many ladies who followed the mob from the jail, and by others who joined it on the terraces nearby.

7

Rise of the scientific spirit in the Bible Belt, as reported in a dispatch from Jackson, seat of Milsaps College, a leading Methodist place of learning, and of the State government of Mississippi:

Albert Brunson, a Negro, who was taken from officers last night by a party of masked men, was returned here today from Clinton, where he was found after his release from his captors, who performed an operation upon him.

8

From the archives of the Committee on the Judiciary of the House of Representatives, in charge of the Dyer anti-lynching bill:

Ashland, Miss.: An unnamed colored man, charged with stabbing a white man, was taken from jail by a mob, hanged, and his body riddled with bullets. The white man, who had charged the Negro with stealing, attempted to search him.

Pickens, Miss.: An 18-year-old colored girl was shot by a mob which was in search of her brother, who was said to have borrowed 50 cents from a white man and refused to pay him 10 cents interest.

9

From an address to the Kiwanis Club of Columbus, a rising town on the Tombigbee river, by the Rev. W. F. Powell, a gifted exhorter of those parts:

God was the first Kiwanian.

10

The qualifications of a candidate for the judicial ermine in rural Mississippi, as described by the learned Cold-water *Herald*:

> Several years ago the Winona Baptist Church, of which he has been a member from boyhood, elected him a deacon, and he is now the efficient superintendent of the Sunday-school of that church, in which capacity he has served three years. He is also a past master of the Winona Masonic Lodge, over which he has presided three years. He was presiding officer also several years in the Lodge of Odd Fellows. He is now council commander of the Winona Camp of Woodmen of the World, and has been for 12 years, or more. He is clerk of the local camp of the Modern Woodmen of America.

11

Editorial amenities in the Hookworm Belt, as revealed by a leading editorial in the Jackson *Free Lance*:

> Our attention has just been called to a recent . . . editorial . . . appearing in the Hazlehurst *Courier* . . . in which it is stated that ex-Governor Bilbo . . . demanded $30,000 to secure a pardon for Will Sorsby from Gov. Russell. . . . The statement is a willful, perjurious and damnable lie. The party who originated this pusillani-mous story ought to be branded with a red-hot iron on the front part of his noodle with the letter " L," so that all truthful and decent people would have advanced warning of the character of the party with whom they were dealing.

MISSOURI

I

Specimen of the oratorical style of the Hon. Elliott Wool-folk Major, ex-Governor of Missouri, from his address at the dedication of the new State Capitol at Jefferson City:

This structure is the product of the best there is in materials and in architecture. The Masterhand is present everywhere, from its golden dome kissing the blue and bending skies, to its foundation, as everlasting as the eternal hills. It is but a child in the life of the State, an administrative infant of two full terms; it never knew swaddling clothes, it was born a giant. It is equalled only by the people of Missouri and the splendid citizenship of the City of Jefferson. This is its abiding place and here it will remain as long as the will of the sovereign people is the will of the land. When a century has laid its hand upon this gibraltar of capitol buildings; when the snows of many Winters have wrapped their white mantles about it; when the Summers' suns shall have kissed them into sparkling waters again, still, this structure will remain a proud testimonial to the past and a glorious herald to the future.

2

Sinister advertisement in the Marshfield *Mail,* a leading public journal of the Ozark region:

COME GET THE REST

Notice to chicken thieves now stealing chickens in Sand Springs neighborhood, and those that stole my flock of Buffs, left five of the flock they did not get, so am cordially inviting them to come and get the rest.

And right here personally guarantee should we by chance meet in my yard or vicinity, that I will not have you arrested or make any complaint for your joke. Am a firm believer in justice, and think should we meet, we can adjust this chicken transaction all by ourselves and be Sheriff, Judge, and Jury, undertaker if necessary. So do not be offish, or wait for any formalities, but just come and make your call any night you think it will suit you. The bull dog will be tied up down in the cellar. The old shot gun spiked in good old Kentucky style, no lock on the hen house door, and everything else in shape accordingly for your benefit and reception. Why hesitate? Come and get the other five, and be welcomed.

W. L. VAN ECK, R. F. D. 1.

3

The Higher Learning at the State university, as described by the Columbia *Missourian:*

With men students of the university, the best selling magazines are *Judge* and the humorous magazines of a risque character. The *Whizz-Bang* seems to be the most popular, although it is said at one news-stand that nearly every university boy who comes in to buy a magazine ends by buying *Ziff's*, which is modeled after the *Whizz-Bang*. Stephens and Christian College girls, university girls and town girls like *True Confessions* or *True Stories* and furnish a large demand for these two magazines.

4

Revival of beautiful letters reported by a new publishing house in Kansas City:

If you enjoy *real* literature—a *Mental Feast*—a *Soul Banquet*—something that will make you bounce a little —a book that you'll call *Sweetheart* before you get half through it, you should read *The Fool-Killer's* new book, " *Warm Wireless Waves.*" There's no book like it in human literature; it reaches mental heights of transcendent beauty and intellectual splendor that no other book ever dreamed of. It's the book you'll want to keep in the family and hand down to future generations. You'll want your wife and children to read it and *live* it. It shakes hands with your *heart* and calls you *pal*. Forty-five *sizzling* pages of *Soul-Music* and *Mental-Cream*. Contains the latest picture of the *Author*. Only 25c a copy or 5 for $1.00. Sent by mail, prepaid.

5

From the esteemed *Globe-Democrat's* summary of a speech before the St. Louis Kiwanis Club by Col. W. C. Archer, a gifted sociologist of Washington, D. C.:

He said civilization today is merely working back to the heights reached by Babylon, Greece and Rome, heights which have only been approximated. He declared the attention given to sanitation by these great cities of the past, as shown by the ruins of water systems, baths and sewers, was the true index of their civilization.

Babe Ruth, and the American athletes who captured most of the honors in the Olympic games, were products of the American shower bath, he declared. Col. Archer said the Russian Communist uprising, from whose effects Europe is still suffering, would never have occurred if Russian homes had been equipped with bath tubs and other sanitary appliances.

6

Official effort to civilize the natives of Johnson county, as reported by the Warrensburg *Star-Journal*:

John Burnett, in charge of the court house, asks that all who attend the band concert tonight be careful and not pull up the grass. Much damage has been done to the lawn by people pulling up the grass while they listen to the concert.

7

Missouri's contribution to the American roster of new and unprecedented crimes, as reported by the St. Louis *Star*:

Patrolman Charles Brockhausen related how he had arrested a " suspicious character " in the Sprague Hotel.
" He acted nervous," the policeman said, " and wanted to rent a room. He said he had been thrown out of his house by his father-in-law. I thought that was funny, so I pinched him."

8

Scientific police methods in St. Louis, as described by the eminent *Times*:

William Lashley, a Negro, was reported by the police yesterday to have admitted shooting to death Lieut.

Sidney E. Sears of the police force. It now appears that Lashley made this "confession" after he had been knocked unconscious with a gun butt, had his jaw broken, three ribs fractured, and had been kicked in the face and stomach and otherwise manhandled. After all these things were done to him, he says, he was asked about the shooting.

9

News item from the Columbia Evening *Missourian*, laboratory newspaper of the University of Missouri's school of journalism:

The football game which Columbia High School was to have played with Sedalia High School tomorrow has been postponed to Monday, at 3 o'clock, because of the death of R. M. Wyatt, janitor at the high school. Mr. Wyatt was a leader in the Rocheport race riot. During the fighting he was shot in the head.

10

Effects of the art of a new stock company leading man upon the gifted dramatic critic of the illustrious St. Louis *Globe-Democrat*:

The great idea that this writer gathers is that in the high ability of the leading man, Edward Dorney, there was displayed to St. Louis auditors a new actor who is worthy of the traditions of Edwin Booth. . . . Dorney was wonderful. He carried the motif of the play in the palm of his hand. He held and dominated it entirely. . . . Always was he conserved, but when, in a moment where he was touched upon his sympathetic heart and aroused to the realm of passion, then he was superb.

11

Calling out the *Landsturm* against the Devil in Kansas
City, as reported by the United Press:

A world's record for Bible class attendance was set
here yesterday by the men's class of the First Baptist
Church, when 17,833 men jammed Convention Hall.
The Baptist Church here is in a contest with a business
men's class in Long Beach, Calif. The Long Beach
class, according to messages received here, had 9,756
yesterday.

12

Pen portrait of the Hon. Sam Baker, the new governor
of Missouri, in the illustrious St. Louis *Star:*

[The Hon. Mr. Baker] is a man of medium height,
very solidly built, with a noticeably thick neck. His
hair is almost pure white, with a small bald spot on the
back of his head. His complexion is a ruddy pink. In
conversation, his features are immobile, and he often
talks out of the right side of his mouth.

13

Tip for transcontinental automobile tourists from the
Rev. C. H. Swift, pastor of the First Christian Church of
Cape Girardeau:

The bootleggers have our city under their control
and do as they please.

14

Statement by the Pauly Jail-Building Company, of St.
Louis, the foremost concern devoted to that science in the
Republic:

We are receiving many inquiries from county seats.
Prohibition has boomed our business.

15

Progress of the scientific spirit and the new jurisprudence in St. Louis, as reported by the eminent *Star:*

A large man industriously rubbing the head of a smaller man at Broadway and Market Street attracted the attention of Detective Sergt. Behnken.

" Do you feel the relief? " asked the large man. The small man announced that he did not, and in addition demanded help, aid and succor. " What is this? " inquired Behnken.

" Very simple," said the large man. " This poor fellow has demons. I am taking them out of him."

" Have you got demons? " asked Behnken.

" I have not," said the small man. " This bird grabbed me as I was walking down the street and began to rub my head."

Behnken settled the matter by giving the demon hunter a swift kick.

16

Rural Missouri's contribution to the theory and practice of the New Journalism, as reported in a dispatch from St. Joe:

Announcement of the consolidation of the Andrew County *Democrat* and the Savannah *Reporter* (Republican), both published at Savannah, Missouri, was made recently. Of opposite political faiths, both papers have been published weekly for many years. Hereafter the *Democrat-Reporter* will be published semi-weekly, one issue to advocate Democratic principles and the other to advance Republican principles.

17

Letter received, according to the *Journal* of the American Medical Association, by the editor of a St. Louis health column:

> *Dear Sir:* Kindly give initials and address of a reliable physician who performs abortions in the *Globe-Democrat* medical column. I am a busy woman and cannot afford to raise a family. Thanks for any information.

18

Brave attempt of St. Louis to make the country forget the shutting down of the breweries, as reported by the estimable *Globe-Democrat:*

> St. Louis district now produces more commercial horseradish roots than the combined acres of all other sections of the United States. With favorable weather and marketing conditions, 500 carloads of roots are shipped during a season.

19

Human progress under the Nineteenth Amendment in St. Louis, as described by a dispatch in the estimable New York *Times:*

> Her thirteenth divorce was granted to Mrs. Cora Yates in the City Court today. Witnesses testified that her husband, Alexander Yates, had been unfaithful. In the same court, on December 11 last, Mrs. Yates obtained a divorce from Albert Lilley, to whom she had been married three times. He was found guilty of extreme and repeated cruelty. Before her first marriage to Lilley the woman had been wedded to nine different

men, and in the course of her marital career she has answered to the names of Walker, Truxler, Joyce, Barnes, Butcher, Crow, Whitney, Lilley, Porter, Swanson and Yates.

20

Domestic life in the mail order and infant damnation regions, as reported in a news dispatch from Houston:

Mrs. Fred Funkey is near death from a shotgun wound, her son, Fred Funkey, Jr., 22, is in a critical condition from knife wounds, and her husband, 65, is badly cut over the face and hands and is under arrest as a result of a free for all family fight Wednesday at their home near Arroll, in which a daughter, Lola, 17, also engaged. The argument is said to have started in a disagreement as to where the family should spend a holiday. The mother and children wanted to go up the creek for a picnic and the father wanted to go down the creek. Funkey is alleged to have shot his wife in the back with a shotgun loaded with two ball bearings. Funkey then was attacked by his son, who was wounded by a large knife cut which severed one rib. Coming to her brother's rescue, Lola beat the father off with a heavy plank.

MONTANA

1

The last word in science, imparted to the Helena *Record-Herald* by Dr. J. R. Collinson, a celebrated Montana chiropractor:

> The neurocalometer is an instrument the function of which is the detection of heat along the spine for the purpose of detecting the location and extent of nerve pressure.

2

Lamentable triumph of Error and Mortal Mind in the sheep country, as reported by the distinguished *Missoulian*, of Missoula:

> Christian Science services in memory of Mrs. John Johnson, who died yesterday afternoon after swallowing Paris green, will be held at the family home this afternoon at 4 o'clock.

3

Contribution to journalistic English by the Helena *Independent*:

> An orchestra dispelled music . . .

NEBRASKA

1

Progress of the New Jurisprudence in the Foreign Missions Belt, as described by the Campbell *Citizen*:

A law was enacted by the Legislature of 1923, making it the duty of poultry dealers to keep a registry of every batch of poultry purchased, showing the date of purchase, the name of the buyer, and the number and breed of the fowls. The purpose of the law is to enable the tracing of stolen poultry and to prevent the sale of an occasional hen that may be enticed from its flock by the youngsters about the alleys. At the present time the Governor is calling attention of law enforcement officers to the lack of observance of this law.

2

Social note from the same instructive journal:

The children of Mr. and Mrs. A. L'Heureux, or a majority of them at least, to the extent of eight boys and three girls, with the families of such of them as are married, making, when assembled, a rather formidable crowd, gave their mother the surprise of her life Saturday evening when they descended upon the parental home to help celebrate her fifty-seventh birthday anniversary. Ma was doing up the housework when the invaders arrived and Pa had taken off his boots to ease his corns and was listening to " Dream Daddy " on the radio, but the program was immediately changed and the evening was spent in hilarity and feasting from the laden baskets with which the children were well provided. It was an occasion long to be remembered.

3

Contribution to the American language by the eminent Plattsmouth *Journal*:

Miss Mia and Barbara Gering very pleasantly entertained on Saturday evening at a *dinnering*.

4

Proud boast of the Hon. Edgar Howard, LL.B., Representative in Congress from the third Nebraska district:

No man or woman in our Nebraska has ever read in a Nebraska newspaper the published statement that any Nebraska woman was getting ready for the visit of the stork. In our clean Nebraska atmosphere such a publication as that would be regarded as unclean.

5

Great statesmen doing their stuff, as reported in the renowned Sioux City *Journal*:

The house of representatives by a rising vote congratulated Wayne (Big) Munn for taking the world's heavyweight wrestling title from Strangler Lewis.

6

Dignified editorial protest in *Awgwan*, the students' paper at the University of Nebraska:

One of the prominent executives of the University, in speaking to a student group, told three successive stories which members of the audience recognized as coming from *Captain Billy's Whiz Bang.* This is a deplorable condition, indeed. This is not the kind of leadership that the parents of Nebraska's ten thousand students would want them to have. *Whiz Bang* may be all right for students to read, but the faculty and executives ought at least to have enough taste to read *Punch* or *Judge.*

NEVADA

I

From a lift of New Thought centres in the eftimable *Nautilus:*

    Reno, Nevada—Radiance Center of Love; Geo. Miller, sec.; Saturno Hotel.

NEW HAMPSHIRE

I

Progress of political science in the colleges, as revealed by the *Daily Dartmouth*:

> An original Coolidge Stampede will be held in Webster Hall tonight. . . . The second speaker will be Miss Ruth Hovey, star of the " Up She Goes " company. Miss Hovey . . . will speak on " How Coolidge Appears to an Actress " . . . Miss Hovey has been termed the prettiest girl in New York.

2

Preaching the Gospel in the ancient town of Kittery, as reported by the *Portsmouth Times*:

> In the pulpit editorial next Sunday evening at the Second M. E. Church the pastor will give a brief outline of the origin and development of the Republican party. You will want to hear it.

3

The passing of a New Hampshire worthy, as reported by the learned *Express*, of Portland, Maine:

> James Somers died suddenly while attending mass at St. Mary's Catholic Church yesterday morning. Mr.

Somers conducted a barber shop on Central avenue twenty-five years. He was the man who shaved Harry K. Thaw when the latter was in New Hampshire as a fugitive from the Matteawan Asylum.

NEW JERSEY

1

From a public bull by the Rev. J. Gresham Machen, D.D., of Princeton Theological Seminary:

The public testimony of Dr. Fosdick, of the First Presbyterian Church, New York, and of the many preachers like him, is . . . producing a confidence in human goodness, in human ability to obey the commands of Christ, which it is the first business of the Christian preacher to break down.

2

Plans and specification for a new religion lately launched by Carl H. Norbrom, 185 North Parkway, East Orange:

1. The church ritual shall be the same as the modern Jewish Synagogue. That of Rabbi Stephen Wise at Carnegie Hall, for example.

2. It shall elect its Rabbi and officers the same as the Christian Science Church.

3. The Old and New Testaments are to be used for texts along with modern science.

4. All members must be total abstainers. No booze.

5. No member of this church may personally sue to recover a debt, nor go into voluntary bankruptcy. He must diversify his investments and use forethought that will prevent his getting into financial difficulties.

6. He must never participate in warfare against

154

another nation, of which 50% of the people are Christians. If conscripted, he must meet the penalty for evasion. He must take a passive attitude toward war propaganda. If a non-Christian country invades his nation, he must help drive them out, but not invade their land.

7. He shall not have a larger family than that which he can afford to raise and educate decently. He should do his utmost to keep his family free from charity.

8. Women to have equal rights with men in all church positions.

9. Owing to the unfairness to the children that follow, the members of one race (color) shall not marry into another, nor shall congregations be mixed in race.

10. No member of this congregation shall ever speak ill of another man's religion.

3

Sad but somehow comforting news from the *Pillar of Fire* of Zarephath, N.J.:

> The Church that God through Wesley launched
>   Two hundred years ago
> Is going now beneath the waves,
>   Down to eternal woe.
>
> She's lost her pow'r to discipline
>   Her pleasure-loving youth—
> Her ministers no longer preach
>   The simple gospel truth.
>
> 'Tis sad indeed to see her sink
>   Into the briny deep,
> Yet naught is there that one can do,
>   But o'er her wreckage weep.

4

Contribution to the Higher Jurisprudence by the learned Porter, J., of the Court of Oyer and Terminer of Essex county, as reported in a news dispatch:

The dying words of an atheist or an unbeliever are inadmissible as evidence in court in New Jersey. On the strength of a precedent established in 1857, Judge Porter refused to admit the testimony of Detective Sergeant Carbally, of Newark, concerning a conversation he had with Thomas R. Loan while Loan was being taken to a hospital after having been shot. " I asked Loan if he wanted a priest or a minister," Carbally said on the stand. " He said he was an atheist and did not want any religious assistance."

5

Proof of a renaissance of the poetic spirit, disclosed in a Trenton dispatch:

CHARTERS FILED

Walt Whitman Garage and Service Co., Camden, . . .; Leroy A. Goodwin, W. Kennedy, C. A. Wolverton, J. J. Scott. . . .

6

Legal notice in the *Burlington County Press* of Riverside:

NOTICE

To Whom It May Concern:

The remark passed by August Rider, Bridgeboro street, on New Year's Eve, that I owed his wife a small sum of money. I wish to state the same has been paid by me, Mrs. Rose Pfeiffer.

7

Entry of Leviticus into the Common Law, as reported from Newark:

Morris Heyman and his wife, of 82 Schuyler avenue, have filed suit in the Essex County Circuit Court for $50,000 against the Castle Ice Cream Company of Irvington. They charged that the company caused them and their guests at their silver wedding anniversary to sin inadvertently. The complaint stated that Heyman ordered twelve bricks of ices from the company to serve his guests and that instead of ices, ice cream was sent. He said that the mistake was not discovered until all had eaten the ice cream, and that, because they had already eaten meat, thus violated a canon of orthodox Jewish law which prohibits eating meat and milk at the same table. Heyman alleged that his guests became indignant when they learned of the mistake and left hurriedly. He said that his clothing business had depreciated as a result of the incident and that his orthodoxy was under suspicion.

8

Improvement in mortuary technic in Camden, as reported by the esteemed *Post-Telegram:*

Funeral Directors B. F. Schroeder & Sons have instituted a new plan in the publishing of death notices. The new departure carries the name of the pastor conducting the service, as well as the name of the church. The new idea has met with the approval of many, according to the phone calls, letters and personal congratulations which have been forthcoming.

9

How Fundamentalism helps Americanization, from the testimony of Sister Buyse, of Jersey City, in the *Apostolic Echo*:

Sixteen years ago, when I came to this country, I couldn't understand a word of English. I went to the Methodist church, and I couldn't understand one word the minister said, but I asked the Lord to help me understand the preaching, and fasted and prayed every Friday. I made it a special plan to fast, so that I could understand the preaching. As I looked at the preacher all I heard sounded like " bubble, bubble, bubble." Then, all at once, I could understand what he said, and I exclaimed " Glory! " and " Praise the Lord! " Those were the first English words I uttered.

10

Solemn warning and defiance of Pastor Charles Hillman Fountain, an eminent ecclesiastic of Plainfield:

Modernism is the most terrible menace to the Church and state that has ever arisen, and we Evangelicals, we Fundamentalists are going to fight it with might and main. We are not going to stop until we have driven every Modernist out of our pulpits and seminaries and editorial chairs. We are going to put them out if it takes our lives to do it.

11

Progress of Law Enforcement in Paterson, as reported in a press dispatch from that great city:

The Women's Independent Republican League of Paterson, at a meeting Monday night, adopted a resolution pledging its entire membership of 100 to the enforcement of "absolute patriotism" among men. They agreed to pay particular attention to military parades, and in every case where a man fails to properly salute the colors to knock his hat from his head.

12

Extract from a history of Christian endeavor, its triumphs and disasters:

The ministers of Jersey City are solidly behind the movement to prevent the holding of the Wills-Firpo fight. They hopefully look to Federal Judge Runyon (a Sunday-school teacher) to issue the warrant charging white slavery against Firpo, an act which would prevent the holding of the fight. Should their hopes prove vain, every one of these ministers will spend the day in earnest prayer for rain. An answer to their prayer would compel the postponement of the fight by the promoters.

13

Wholesale triumph of the True Faith in the remote fastnesses of the State, as described by the illustrious New York *World*:

The entire population of Samptown, N.J., a mill community five miles from Plainfield, had been "captured" and enrolled under the Salvation Army flag. The population of Samptown totals 159, of whom 80 per cent. work in the steel mill of George Harris. There is a mixture of several nationalities, including Italians, Hungarians and Spaniards. Mr. Harris decided religious influence was needed to dispel racial antipathies. At his invitation, the Salvation Army in Plainfield sent men to Samptown about a month ago and held a meeting, at which sixteen adults announced their conversion. At the second meeting, a week later, ninety men, women and children joined. At the third meeting, a few nights ago, thirty-eight more came forward. Converts brought in the remaining fifteen of the population.

14

Revival of medieval measures against heresy among the Fundamentalists of Morristown, as reported by the public prints:

Publications of the Christian Science and Unitarian churches, and those dealing with the teachings of Pastor Russell were burned in an incinerator at the conclusion of a gospel meeting last night, conducted by Charles Winters, evangelist. A group of women stood by the incinerator and sang hymns while " Science and Health," the Christian Science hymnal, the *Unitarian Leader*, Forbish's " Life of Christ," and other works were burned.

NEW MEXICO

I

Judicial remarks of Leahy, J., of the District Court at Albuquerque, delivered from the bench during the hearing of the case of The State vs. Magee:

It remained for you [Magee], a political harlot from the State of Oklahoma, to come here and make these charges against me. I use the term " political harlot " advisedly. . . .

You published an editorial from another paper headed " Resign." The editor of that paper, like you, is also a political harlot from the same place. I might add, in addition, that he is a fat-headed semi-imbecile, incapable of earning a living. . . .

You [Magee] have shown yourself to be a low down —I was about to say skunk; but there is this difference between you and a skunk. A skunk has a white stripe on his back and there is nothing white about you. You are merely a mangy yellow cur. . . .

2

Melancholy advertisement in the amiable Santa Fé *Public Voice:*

PUBLIC NOTICE

Since my wife of two weeks, Mrs. Zetta Chamber-Goins-Root, has decided to stay in Santa Rosa and look after her own needs with no regard for my interests,

I give notice that I will not be held responsible for anything she says, does or contracts for.

W. G. Root.

3

Warning to virgins posted in the Y.W.C.A. at Albuquerque:

Remember that these diseases can be contracted from kissing or dancing with a man who is diseased. . . . Never forget that at least 25 per cent, *or one out of every four* men whom you know are diseased.

NEW YORK

1

Official pronunciamento by the Hon. John L. Reilly, president of the Schenectady Rotarians:

Lincoln was a born Rotarian; born ahead of time. . . . The spirit of Lincoln is the spirit of Rotary.

2

Sign hanging in the studio of an eminent Manhattan chirotonsor:

After the hair is cut it should be singed in order to close up the ends. This prevents your catching a cold in the head through the open ends of the hairs.

3

Notice in the programme of the Knickerbocker Theatre, New York City:

The following are three continual complaints from our patrons:
1. Throwing garments over the backs of seats into others' laps.
2. Kicking, keeping time to music and using the seat in front for a foot rest.
3. Combing bobbed hair outside the dressing room. This is unhealthy and is DEPRECATED BY THE HEALTH DEPARTMENT.

4

Specimen of the Washington correspondence set before the metropolitan Babbittry by the eminent New York *Times*:

It muſt have dawned on the country that Mr. Coolidge's reticence is self-inflicted. He has a retentive memory and powers of suſtained application built upon an extraordinarily quick and perceptive mind. The hundreds of ſtories of his casual repartee—when he cares to indulge—exclude any other conclusion.

Recently on a particularly busy morning—it was Cabinet day, press conference day and during the delegation hour to boot—the author of a Coolidge biography put into the President's hand a copy of the volume. The President flashed:

" When I get more time I'll write you a book review."

That he talks in several different languages applicable to the person present is indicated by the fact that he did not say he would write an analysis, or a literary criticism, but that he used the trade phrase, " book review." Furthermore, the idea of the President carefully analyzing a 270-page sketch of himself and suggeſting that he write his opinion of the author's opinion of him is not without its undercurrent of humor.

5

Progress of liberty in the Republic, as revealed in the illuſtrious *Herald-Tribune*:

Mr. Lewis introduced a resolution which was adopted: *Resolved*, by the National Republican Club, That the penal law of the State of New York be so amended as to make it unlawful for any person within the ſtate of

New York, not a citizen of the United States and a resident of this State, to print, publish or advocate orally the abolition or amendment of the Constitution of the United States or of the State of New York, or to denounce or criticize any public officer of the United States or of any State, or to denounce or criticize any law enacted by the Government of the United States or of any State or of any civil division thereof.

6

Divertissements of the New York literati, as revealed by a postcard sent through the United States mails:

THE AUTHORS' LEAGUE FELLOWSHIP

The April Luncheon will be held at The Town Hall Club Rooms, 123 West 43rd, on Friday, 12:30. $1.50. At 1:30 you will be asked Two Questions: IS PIGS PIGS? by Ellis Parker Bulter. IF THEY IS, How COME? by George Creel. The answers to be given by You voluntarily from the Floor in Three-minute Unfoldments. EVERYBODY, be *sure* to come!

ARTHUR GUITERMAN, *President*
MARAVENE THOMPSON, *Secretary*

7

Lugubrious conclusions of the Rev. John Roach Straton, D.D., the Baptist Pope of New York, as reported by the world-famous *Times:*

Vice and crime are increasing day by day. Sensualism rules supreme on stage and screen. Many magazines and best sellers are putrid with moral iniquity.

The popular dance has descended to the lowest depths of degradation. Churches on every side are lukewarm and spiritually paralyzed, and blatant infidelity is proclaiming its untruths in college halls and even from many pulpits of the land. The marriage vow is becoming a scrap of paper. The foundations of the home have all been destroyed by commercialized amusements and a money-mad, pleasure-crazed race is rushing on toward the precipice!

8

From a public bull by E. F. Albee, the eminent vaudeville magnate:

Vaudeville has accepted Christ's teaching. For the past eight years they have been lived up to by the managers and artists in this branch of the theatrical profession.

9

From an address by Dr. J. H. Hawkins at Oceanside, L.I.:

The way you can tell a Klansman is by looking at a clean, upright man who does not live with another man's wife.

10

Proud boast of the Rev. William Carter, D.D., pastor of the Throop Avenue Presbyterian Church, Brooklyn:

Brooklyn, thank God, is still the City of Churches. Heresies originate in New York, not in Brooklyn. Between us geographically is the East River, but theologically there is something far broader and deeper. Brooklyn still believes in the Bible as the inspired word of God.

11

From an interview with the Hon. John S. Sumner, Secretary of the Society for the Suppression of Vice, in the New York *World:*

The stage last season was the cleanest in years and this season it is the worst in history, according to John S. Sumner:

" It has touched a lower level than ever before," he declared, " both in the exploitation of salacious themes and in the exhibition of nudity. Complaints to the society have been very numerous. Many organizations have shown great interest in the matter."

He said the statement had been made to him *that the moral character of the scene shifters was being imperiled in one or two shows.*

12

Progress of the Higher Learning at Columbia University, from a list of " subjects covered by the Home Study Courses " in a paid advertisement of the university in the estimable *Dial:*

Philosophy
Photoplay Composition
Biblical Literature
Fire Insurance
Foreign Exchange
Greek
Typewriting
Scouting
Composition of Lyric Poetry
Public Speaking
Modern Drama

Sociology
Psychology of Advertising
Latin

13

News item from the humorous *World:*

An international propaganda was organized yesterday at the Bankers' Club to remind the entire world of the merits of the Golden Rule . . . and the membership of a national Golden Rule Committee was announced. It includes . . . General Leonard Wood. . . .

14

Replies recorded by a *Sun* reporter who sought answers in lower Broadway to the question, Should Christianity be debated from a public platform?

1. Frank Mueller, M.D., 100 East Seventy-fourth Street—I am not in favor of any discussion of Christianity on any public platform, especially of the authenticity of the word of God. Modernism and materialism and even the old Babylonian philosophy are being taught in many places in this country.

2. H. Harris, retired business man, 56 Concord Street, Brooklyn—Absolutely no. The Bible, the living word of God, has stood the test of centuries.

3. Turner A. Monroe, accountant, 120 Broadway—I believe that instead of an argument on the truth of the Bible, on a public platform the preachers should teach the gospel as it is written. The Bible will take care of itself.

4. J. C. Clark, restaurateur, 135 West Forty-seventh Street—Everybody has a right to his own opinion. Free speech is allowed in this country, but to discuss on

a public platform the truth of the Bible is going too far. I do not approve of it.

5. P. De Fliese, banking, 120 Broadway—I see no occasion for any debate or discussion as to the truth of the Bible. It is the only record we have, and Christianity stands or falls on its authenticity.

15

Theological dictum from an article in *America* by the Rev. Wilfrid Parsons, S.J.:

How do we know that this particular miracle of the Virgin Birth happened? We know that it happened *because the Catholic Church teaches that it happened.* This is in itself complete, absolute and final proof of the truth of this doctrine.

16

The theatre's tribute to the late Dr. Wilson, from a memoir in *Variety* entitled " The Draped Proscenium ":

During the bitter days of the grim war he was a steady attendant at the lighter amusements. Each Monday found him in his box at Keith's. The players gloried in his presence and he smiled upon them. . . . After the war he modestly declined to use the box he had so long occupied as President, but came each Monday and sat in extra seats behind the last row. A sincere patron of the stage arts, a figure almost divine who lent the glamor of his person to heighten the effulgence of an institution so frequently shadowed by the intolerance of the soulless, Woodrow Wilson glorified the history of the theatre as he glorified the history of his country and his world.

17

Bilious note by the Rev. Dr. Alexander Lyon, rabbi of
the Eighth Avenue Temple, Brooklyn:

If some of the high-salaried rabbis I know of were
judged as they ought to be, not by their dramatic
drawing powers but by the quality and quantity of their
private influence, they would have to work for a living
instead of having others work so that they might talk.
Character outside the pulpit is a greater power for good
than oratory in it.

18

From a half-page pronunciamento in the eminent Buffalo
Courier by the eloquent spokesman of Anglo-Saxon ideals,
the Hon. Armand Boulfrois:

Over here, all true-blooded and sincere Americans
are highly satisfied with the Constitution of the United
States, as set down by our pioneer ancestors, and those
rank outsiders and newcomers who don't like that
Constitution and who won't respect their Uncle Sammy
are informed that ALL AMERICA will gladly welcome
their room in preference to their company. Let them
get out and go back to their land o'er the seas, or to
Russia, or to HELL, or to some new-found land where
they can stir up a special potpourri of their own and stew
in their witches' broth of hate.

These lazy floaters simply worm their way into every
sort of organization for the shady business of churning-
up dissatisfaction among decent, contented, respectable
citizens in the hope that they may cause a governmental
overthrow and cash-in on the resultant plunder. They
have no more regard for a family and home than a
common hobo. They have absolutely no place in

American society and are only keeping YOU from Owning Your Own Home.

19

From an address of the Hon. Otto Kahn, LL.D., at the Harvard Club:

There is no better inveſtment, from the material and every other point of view, than thinking.

20

Patrio-ethical note from the New York *Evening Journal:*

You feel a thrill of American pride when you read of a girl in Chicago, 18 years old, beautiful, earning her living by posing as a model before an art class, who went to another room and took poison " because she was so much ashamed." . . . How many marriage proposals will Chicago's modeſt girl receive if she lives?

21

From an appeal for subscriptions sent out to members of the class of 1920 by their representative on the Columbia University Alumni Fund Committee:

Form the habit of endowing schools now; it may be a valuable one later on.

22

Contribution to the secret hiſtory of the Republic by the Rev. C. Lewis Fowler, editor of the American *Standard:*

President Harding . . . was a thirty-third degree Mason, and though he made some blunders in his appointments, he was awake to a large extent on the Roman Catholic question, and did not respond to their influence as readily as desired. He ... fell ill and passed away. He was not poisoned by food that " disagreed with him," as the press related. He was poisoned mentally, *a victim to the telepathic practises of Jesuit adepts.*

23

Exercise in logic by one of the master-minds of the cinema:

Premise—One thing you can be sure of: When you start out to see a Universal picture, you will *know* it is clean—and good. You will know that the story was written by a popular author and that the cast will be excellent. You will *know* that you can take your children without fear that they will be shocked or made familiar with the world's follies before their time. That's a lot, isn't it? What more could be desired?

Conclusion—Have you seen Champion Jack Dempsey in Universal's " Fight and Win " pictures? I think they're great. What do *you* think?

CARL LAEMMLE
President

24

From a press-sheet announcing the appointment of the Hon. Richard C. Fowler, an eminent Detroit advertising man, to be general manager of the American Viewpoint Society of New York:

At the close of the war he initiated a movement, which received the enthusiastic support of President Harding, to place the American flag at the top of every Christmas tree.

25

Argument against the Darwinian hypothesis of natural selection delivered before the massed Christians of Elmira by the Rev. Dr. Billy Sunday:

If anyone wants to teach that God-forsaken, hell-born, bastard theory of evolution, then let him go out and let him be supported by men who believe that blasted theory and not expect the Christian people of this country to pay for the teaching of a rotten, stinking professor who gets up there and teaches our children to forsake God and makes our schools a clearing-house for their God-forsaken dirty politics.

26

Contribution to Shakespearean criticism by the learned editor of the *Catholic Mind:*

The author of the Shakespeare plays, whoever he was, may very well have been a Catholic, but cannot possibly have been a Protestant. What is the proof? If he were a Protestant, why did he not display his Protestantism? He had every inducement to do so; all his Protestant compeers did it. But he never did. There is no touch of Protestantism in any Shakespearean scenes which are certainly authentic; no attempt to gratify the mob or the Queen with an anti-Catholic fling. . . . The absence of Protestantism in his plays is therefore a strong (if not absolutely conclusive) proof that he was not a Protestant. The absence of definite Catholicism is no proof that he was not definitely a Catholic.

NORTH CAROLINA

I

A late flowering of Christian doctrine among the Fundamentalists, as reported by the Charlotte *Observer:*

Vividly bringing out the similarity between John the
Baptist and Billy Sunday, the Rev. Joseph A. Gaines,
pastor of St. John's Baptist Church, preached at the
evening service Sunday at St. John's Church a powerful
sermon on " There Came a Man."

Billy Sunday is the same type of man as John the
Baptist and as time goes on the world is coming to
place upon him an estimate similar to the one that John
the Evangelist placed upon John the Baptist, declared
Mr. Gaines.

2

Rewards of Christian public servants among the Tar
Heels, as reported by the eminent Smithfield *Herald:*

Editor The Herald:

Last Sunday as we drove past the filling stations and
soft drink stands on our way to church our hearts were
filled with gratitude to God for Mr. N. B. Grantham
and the grand jury as a whole for their action taken in
enforcing the law against Sabbath breaking. We want
to thank them every one and pray God's richest blessing
upon them.

Our Sunday-school gave a rising vote of thanks to
the grand jury.　　　　　　C. L. BATTEN,
Supt. Micro Baptist Sunday-school

174

3

Rise of a new bugaboo among the Tar Heel Baptists, as reported by the Winston-Salem *Journal*:

"With the present movement northward of Negroes," said the Rev. Dr. C. A. Owens in his sermon at the First Baptist Church last night, " and in the absence of a race prejudice that has protected the Southerners, there is the greatest possible danger of the mingling of the races, so that in the future it may come to pass that you will send your daughter to the North for culture and she will come back with a little Negro."

4

From a public bull by the Hon. Cameron Morrison, Governor and Captain-General of all the Tar Heels:

The government of the United States and the constitutional principles of representative government upon which our fabric of free government rests is (*sic*) final and ultimate truth about government on this earth.

5

Effects of a Billy Sunday revival on the North Carolina soul, as shown by a mysterious advertisement in the estimable Charlotte *Observer*:

TAKE IT FROM BILLY SUNDAY

if not from your Uncle Ed: High Society, female cigarettes, liquor drinking, rum selling or booze buying, gambling in anything—cards, golf, futures, " modern " views on religion, do not bring happiness *even* here below, and what they do for your hereafter is Hell.

IF CHARLOTTE WOMEN

were as good as they are beautiful and fascinating and alluring we'd have the best city on earth, and Billy wouldn't be here with his Castor Oil and quinine. Men follow women. Listen to me, Mabel: if you women would cut to the heart the ducks that drink and lie and steal and that don't pay their debts when they can, and that are immoral, we'd have something more valuable than " The greatest church-going town in the world."

HOLD ON NOW, MABEL,

just keep on your shirt—our women are as good as any other women, better than lots, and our men are not the worst—but calomel is a good medicine.

E. L. KESSLER,
Secretary and Treasurer.

6

Re-entrance of the Devil into Charlotte, as reported by the learned *Observer*:

Fifty-eight persons used the reading and reference rooms of the public library between the hours of 2 and 6 o'clock yesterday afternoon, the first Sunday of the Winter that the doors were open. Beginning of the Sabbath evening reading hours was postponed until Billy Sunday left.

Progress of Christian enlightenment in the Saluda Mountains, as described in a dispatch from Henderson to the Hon. Josephus Daniels' paper, the Raleigh *News and Observer*:

A warning and an indictment were sounded by Rev. M. F. Ham, the evangelist, in his sermon before 5,000

people at the Ham-Ramsay tabernacle Sunday afternoon, when he preached on " The Present-Day Offensive of the Anti-Christ." This anti-Christ he pictured
as a great vice organization that exists in the United
States, fostered and fathered by the Third Internationale
of the Soviet government at Moscow. He denounced it
and warned his audience against its insidious, secret
workings.

It was one of the most stirring addresses, or sermons,
ever heard in this city, and was featured by the reading
of excerpts of discoveries made by United States secret
service men in literature seized in the raid upon the
communist meeting at Bridgeman, Mich. Mr. Ham
charged that this organization was working through
its support of the liquor traffic, the white slave trade,
through fostering sports and games in colleges and
high schools, by means of the dance, corrupt literature,
the incessant demand of the people for luxuries, in its
aim at destroying family life, in Russian relief drives,
false philosophies, and the like. This organization he
characterized as the work of the anti-Christ.

Mr. Ham declared that this international organization aims at devitalizing Christianity and forcing an
economic situation which will bring on a revolution,
and that upon the ruins of the government will be built
the kingdom of the anti-Christ, which will be dominated
for a time by Satan and later will be broken up when
Christ comes to reign.

8

Contribution to human knowledge by the learned editor
of the Charlotte *Observer*, the leading family paper between the Wateree and Yadkin rivers

The Bible which lies open upon every Masonic altar

should be a reminder to every Mason of the sense of his obligation, and an incentive to comply so much as lies within his power to keep and perform the duties he has promised to do. Without the Bible upon the altar of a Masonic lodge, there would be no Masonic lodge. From its pages every thought, relative to the world's progress, has been derived. All Masonry is a sacred college of instruction, filled with divine inspiration. Each degree reveals to the discerning eye a delightful surprise.

9

Sinister notice in the instructive weekly paper of the town of Snow Hill:

There is a certain married man in Snow Hill who is paying too much attention to a little girl—a girl just upon the brink of womanhood. We are confident that his intentions are anything but honorable. We are not naturally suspicious—but what we have seen, we have seen. So far we are sure no harm has been done—but disaster lies just around the corner. Unless this man desists from his hellish purpose we shall consider it our duty to inform the parents of the girl—and we shall perform that duty. Watch your step, libertine!

10

Specimen of the classical, or orgiastic variety of North Carolina prose, from a Greensboro dispatch to the Raleigh *News and Observer*:

Young men with their faces set toward the future, with a vision of the kingdoms of this earth becoming the kingdoms of the Lord; middle-aged men who have bearing upon their shoulders the brunt of the battles of the cross at the present time, gray-haired ministers who have through the years made noble stands for the faith that is within them and are now ready for their mantle to fall upon younger and stronger men, and old veterans in the cause of Christ, leaning upon staffs, who through the decades gone were bulwarks of strength in their struggle against the powers of darkness but because of age and infirmities have been forced from the active ranks of the ministry, all filed down the aisles of West Market Street Church today to enter together upon the duties and responsibilities of the thirty-fifth annual session of Western North Carolina Conference which convened at 9 o'clock in the Mother Church of Methodism in Guilford county.

II

Results of a questionnaire sent to students at the University of North Carolina by the editor of the *Carolina Magazine*:

Cases	No. of different girls had dates with during Summer	Tried to neck	Necked	Necked at first attempt
1	17	17	14	13
2	8	1	1	1
3	2	2	1	1
4	1	—	—	—
5	5	3	3	0
6	4	2	1	0
7	6	3	3	3
8	12	5	5	5
9	6	6	5	4

Cases	No. of different girls had dates with during Summer	Tried to neck	Necked	Necked at first attempt
10	13	5	4	—
11	1	—	—	—
12	0	0	0	0
13	8	4	4	0
14	8	1	1	1
15	1	—	—	—
16	14	7	7	4
17	7	1	1	1

The average number of girls each man had dates with was about 6; the average number of girls each tried to have a petting party with was about 4; and the average number of girls petted was slightly less than 4. Thus 87.7% of those tried were necked.

12

Upward sweep of the Fundamentalist wave from the steppes of Texas toward the line of the Potomac, as revealed by a dispatch from Raleigh:

The North Carolina State Board of Education, headed by Governor Cameron Morrison, today voted to bar from the list of biologies to be adopted by the State high schools all books which in any way intimate an origin of the human race other than that described in the Bible. " Evolution," said Governor Morrison, " means progress, but it does not mean that man, God's highest creation, is descended from a monkey or any other animal. I will not allow any such doctrine or intimation of such doctrine to be taught in our public schools."

13

Effects of the war for democracy, as reported in a dispatch from Goldsboro:

> Allen Moses and his wife, wealthy Negroes, left here in Pullman berths tonight for Washington and New York. This is the first time in the history of this city that Negroes have " had the nerve," as one citizen expressed it, to buy sleeper tickets here. White citizens are aroused, and it is said the Ku Klux Klan will be asked to give Moses a warm reception on his return.

14

Mysterious workings of the Holy Spirit in the bogs along the coast, as described in a dispatch from Wilmington to the Raleigh *News and Observer:*

> Untouched by human hand, the siren on the death car in which Leon George and Sam Lilly rode to their doom in the Brunswick swamps sounded incessantly this morning at the exact hour a jury in the Brunswick Superior Court was bringing in a verdict of guilty against the alleged slayers, according to Captain N. J. Williams, chief of the detective squad at the local police department. So incessant was the blast of the horn, the police official declared, that it was necessary for the police mechanician to sever the wires connecting the horn with the battery to silence the clamor. The machine at the time was in the police yard to the rear of the city hall. Half a dozen policemen corroborated the story.

15

The campaign for Law Enforcement along the Cape Fear river, as reported by the esteemed Winston-Salem *Union-Republican*:

A couple of Prohibition enforcement officers hired a jitney driver at Dunn, Harnett county, to take them on a trip a few days ago and while out made it known that they would like to have some whisky and persuaded the driver to get it for them. As a result of his kindness they arrested him for retailing and transporting.

16

Effects of the *Bookman* School upon literary criticism in Charlotte, as revealed by the eminent *Observer* of that city:

He is a student of Yale and becomes a poet of reputation. He falls madly in love with the heartless, soulless beauty, Inez Martin, who finally jilts him. After she does this he loses every atom of decency, and sins and sins until the reader is so disgusted that he wants to throw the book away, but curiosity seizes him to see whether or not Jeffrey's illicit desires will ever cease. . . .

When Darwin was thinking up something to claim kin with, I can't imagine why he selected the ape instead of a faith-intelligent and appealing little dog.

17

Exchange of amenities between church and State in North Carolina, as reported by a news dispatch from Raleigh:

The ball room of the governor's mansion was the

scene of a prayer service this afternoon, when more than
100 people, mostly State officials and employes and their
wives, attended services conducted by the Rev. M. F.
Ham. The evangelist highly praised Governor Morrison for the character of his administration, mentioning
specifically the action of the executive in throwing out
books on evolution from the accredited list of school
books.

18

Bitter reflection of the editors of the *Carolina Magazine*,
organ of the more literate students at the State university:

North Carolina has less alien blood per square inch
than any other State in the Union. That is one good
reason why she also has less writers, less painters, less
sculptors, and, above all, less musicians than practically
any other State of equal resource; certainly any other
State of equal bombast.

19

High, hot words of the Hon. Isaac M. Meekins, of
Elizabeth City, an eminent Federal judge:

As the shepherd loves the flock he leads afield, so he,
in whose heart his countrymen are enshrined, serves
and leads them best. Never to tire; never to grow cold;
to look for the budding flower and the opening heart;
to hope always; to love always,—this is service; this
is duty; and Calvin Coolidge is all SERVICE—all
DUTY.

20

Rise of an intellectual aristocracy in North Carolina, as reported by a Charlotte correspondent of the New York *World:*

North Carolinians read the *World* and they even read the editorial, theatre and literary pages. A day or so ago I commented on the work of Mr. Heywood Broun in a column I conduct on a country newspaper, and immediately thereafter I was stopped on the streets by several of the townspeople, who discussed Broun with me. They read his column and his reviews and liked him. They also read " The Conning Tower " and the gardens of verses offered therein. Some of them go so far as to read Deems Taylor's talk about the music world. The sophisticates hereabout keep as close tab on the movement in the theatre district as do the smartest of New Yorkers. Then when they take their annual pilgrimage to the city they march down Broadway with a most supercilious air and are thoroughly entertained.

21

From a public statement by the Hon. W. F. Cooper, superintendent of the Southern Railway at Salisbury:

Nothing gives me more pleasure than to be able to testify to the wonderful results which I have been able personally to observe of the " Billy " Sunday Campaigns in our southern States. As you doubtless know, the Southern Railway has thousands of employés located in the cities of Spartanburg, Columbia and Charleston, S.C., and Charlotte, N.C. All of the above places have had " Billy " within the past 18 months. From a purely worldly standpoint, he and his faithful band of co-workers have been worth millions of dollars to our company, for, as you know, Christian men make the best employés, and we know hundreds have been led to Christ through this servant of God. As for my own experience, " Billy " Sunday has helped me, and I am trying to help others. We are making the religion of the Lord Jesus real on the Southern Railway.

22

The struggle for complete righteousness among the Tar Heels, as revealed by a dispatch from Raleigh:

Flirting with college girls or teachers will be outlawed in North Carolina by a measure now before the State Senate committee on education. The bill classes flirting as a misdemeanor, punishable with a fine of not less than five nor more than fifty dollars or imprisonment for not less than ten nor more than thirty days. It applies to the school buildings, roads and sidewalks used as routes to and from school.

NORTH DAKOTA

I

Handbill diſtributed among the freemen of the rising town of Harvey by Paſtor Albert H. Crombie:

Fellow Citizens:

Everybody knows that it is the work of Miniſters of the Gospel to preach againſt and fight sin—not simply piĉture the joys of heaven for the few. I'm not much good at preaching about the sins of Jerusalem or Moses but I try to preach praĉtical sermons againſt the sins of Harvey and her Citizens. And so—in the CON-GREGATIONAL CHURCH—

Next Sunday Night—at 7.30 o'Clock Sharp, I am Going to Preach the Plainest, Straightest and Hottest Sermon About the Sins of Harvey that I Know How to Preach.

Judge what it will be like by my sermons on dancing, card playing, movies and tobacco. I haven't room here to tell you much about it but if you want to know what my subjeĉt will be—here it is:

" under the lid of harvey—the sins of our city."

In that sermon I am going to tell you about the Officers and certain Citizens of our City and show you juſt what people believe is going on, such as home brewing—bootlegging—gambling—cigarette selling—*and worse things*. I'm not going to abuse anyone but I'm going to try to show you the real Harvey—the City that blind-

186

folded the Governor of the State and fooled the Soo Railroad Officials and made them believe that Harvey is a decent city.

You have heard the gossip—I challenge you to come out and hear the facts. If you love God and hate the devil—or vice versa—come early and get a good seat.

Don't forget the place and date and come if you think I will deliver the goods. CONGREGATIONAL CHURCH SUNDAY NIGHT.

REV. ALBERT H. CROMBIE.

2

Effects of the Americanization movement on the steppes, as reported by the eminent Fargo *Tribune*:

Paul Salzberger, Fargo, cousin of Fritz Kreisler, will not hear his celebrated kinsman when he plays here Tuesday evening, because, as he explains it, the Improved Order of Red Men meets that night. Mr. Salzberger is secretary of the lodge.

OHIO

The process of training an Ohio literatus, as described by the Cincinnati *Enquirer*:

Mr. Jack Withrow, who has decided upon a literary career, for which his friends and associates predict a brilliant future, is now steeping himself in the beauty and romance of Southern France after some months in Paris, where he has been studying at the Sorbonne. He took his M.A. at Harvard after graduating at Williams College, and that his field of self-expression is to be that of the short story is interesting in that this background of culture, as well as his inheritance of facile humor and apt craftsmanship, will bring to that literary genre a vivid comprehension of types that should be of moment in shaping his own prospects and in giving to the output of at least one of the younger generation of writers, with which he is now to be included, something more than a facility for the slang of the period, however amusingly portrayed and enormously capitalized. Mr. Withrow, who is the elder son of Dr. and Mrs. J. M. Withrow, has been enjoying immensely the palmy shores of the Mediterranean, and, being ensconced in one of the quaint picture-book villages near Cannes, where he is in touch with the flowery paths of dalliance, as well as the native beauty of the famous Riviera, he has had ample opportunity to find himself. He was part of the Mardi Gras fete of flowers, always a moment of picturesque importance in European life, and his wanderings up and down the historic shell road that outlines the blue waters at this point have given him an insight into the great world of human nature that has made his impressions replete with vivid images.

2

Workings of the constitutional safeguard against double jeopardy in Ohio, as described in a Cleveland dispatch to the Columbus *State Journal:*

After serving six months in the Mahoning county jail at Youngstown on a charge of possession of intoxicating liquor, Joe Romo, of Youngstown, was given an additional 30-day sentence when arraigned before Federal Judge Westenhaver here today. He will serve his sentence in the Canton workhouse. Romo, the evidence showed, possessed one quart of home made wine when arrested.

3

Contribution to the American language from Cincinnati, as reported by the esteemed *Enquirer:*

What has caused the most comment is the autoria, or place for automobiles, a new word coined by Mrs. Dill, who believes that the word garage brings visions of oil stations and is perhaps not quite so refined as autoria.

4

From a florid exposure of a congress of Reds in the *Ohio Journal of Commerce*, the official organ of the Buckeye Babbitts:

Great Britain was represented by its Port Laureat, Elvin Markham.

189

5

From a report of the deliberations of the Savings Division of the Investment Bankers Association, lately in session at Cleveland:

> Delegates to the division were advised by Ruth Roland, motion picture star, to cultivate the friendship of the boys and girls as a practical method of promoting thrift.

6

Contribution to sociology by the editor of the distinguished Toledo *Blade:*

> There are many definitions of a hick town. We don't like the phrase, but to our mind a hick town is a community where half the women count backwards when the first baby arrives in the home of a newly-married couple.

7

Progress of penology at the Ohio Penitentiary, as reported by the *Northern Review*, the official newspaper of the Ohio Northern University:

> I made it a point to visit the penitentiary and was informed in the presence of Warden Thomas that 95 per cent of the 2,800 prisoners incarcerated there at this time use tobacco. But they do not smoke cigarettes, for Warden Thomas will not permit a cigarette within the prison walls.

8

Hardships of a Christian pastor in the Lake Erie littoral, as reported by the Rev. T. Howard Jones, of Lorain:

ARE YOU IN FAVOR OF THIS?

1. Conducting a sly, sneaking, false propaganda to destroy the reputation of the minister.

2. Calling two hundred new members—good Christian people,—" Trash! "—threatening to shoot the preacher in the Church.

3. Refusing to pay the minister his salary; even when the people contributed it for the minister.

4. In the Church, about the altar, hissing during prayer; yelling in public service, " liar! " tearing the clothing of the preacher and cursing him on Sunday in the Church; fighting and spilling blood at the altar over the possession of the money given to our Christ.

5. When the pastor resigned, within twenty-four hours, the minister was ordered to get out of the parsonage; an officer of the church entering the parsonage kitchen and talking shamefully to the pastor's family.

6. The flat refusal—and they still refuse—to pay the preacher the $200.00 due Dr. Jones today. Yet they employed a lawyer and served legal notice, giving the preacher two days to get out at once.

If you are in favor of the above things taking place in a church then you ought to stay with, attend, pay and pray for the Twentieth St. M. E. Church.

9

Fashion note from a booklet issued by a Cleveland hotel:

A man may wear a red necktie, a green vest and tan shoes, and still be a gentleman.

191

10

Specimen 100% dithyrambs from the *Rhythmic World*,
the organ of the New Poetry Movement in Cincinnati:

TO ARMS! To arms! To arms! To arms!
Rise ye, end all the alarms.
Hesitate no longer to fight;
Rise ye, conquer in the right.

CHORUS:

Patriots, hear your Country call you;
Rise ye, loyal, good and true.
To arms! To arms! To arms!
Patriots, now, your country needs you;
Rise ye, loyal, good and true.
To arms! To arms! To arms!

March on! March on! March on! March on!
Battles wait you to be won.
Render service in the army;
Train ye, for the victory.

Sail on! Sail on! Sail on! Sail on!
Rise ye, every loyal son.
Render service in the navy;
Win the fight for liberty.

On, carry on! On, carry on!
Joined together, all as one.
In the army, navy, all true;
Thus, your Country, now, needs you.

11

From a propagandist address by the Hon. William Clendenin before the annual meeting of the American Kraut Packers' Association at Cincinnati:

Sauerkraut contains more alcohol than the $\frac{1}{2}$ of 1% that the Volstead Act permits in beverages. The alcohol in it ranges from .72 of 1% to well over 1%. These figures come from the experts of the University of Wisconsin.

12

Brotherly love among the Cleveland Wesleyans, as disclosed by the eminent *Plain Dealer:*

It is a friendly place, this Windermere Methodist Episcopal Church. A stranger will have to be an artful dodger if he succeeds in getting in or out of the church without a handshake. The minister, Dr. McCarty, is the most confirmed handshaker of all. One may manage to elude him when entering the church, but one will have to find a side door through which to disappear if there is to be escape from his hearty greeting at the close of the service.

13

Bitter protest from the learned and discriminating editorial writer of the *Lookout Magazine of Christian Education* of Cincinnati:

Every college in America is teaching heathenism by having in its curriculum Tacitus, Virgil, Homer, Sophocles, Euripides, Æschylus, Plato and Aristotle. The minute you suggest using the writings of Matthew, Mark, Luke, John, Paul, Isaiah, Jeremiah, Ezekiel or any of the rest of this noble group the education nostrils elevate to the ninetieth degree of altitude. Yet the Christians of America are paying taxes and contributing the money that keep college doors open.

14

Evening diversions among the Cleveland Congregationalists, as reported by the eminent *Plain Dealer:*

"LOVE'S TRIUMPH"

A LECTURE BY DR. H. SAMUEL FRITSCH

How to make love psychologically irresistible. How to overcome adverse conditions and obstacles in love. How to overcome coldness and indifference in the one loved. Consolation for those who have loved and lost. How those who miss love may have all of love's rewards by the practice of sublimation. How love may be unconditionally realized.

This is the final lecture in the course on the Love-Life. Hear it! Souvenir poem.

At the Hough Avenue Congregational Church

15

Joint resolution introduced in the General Assembly of Ohio by the Hon. Mr. Schafer, a Christian statesman:

It shall be the duty of the chaplain of the Senate and House of Representatives, at the opening of each day's session, to read without sectarian comment at least ten verses of the Bible. The reading of such verses of the Bible shall precede the prayer service. It shall be the duty of each member and employé of the General Assembly, and of each newspaper correspondent who has been accorded the privileges of the two houses, to commit to memory the Ten Commandments and the Golden Rule.

A committee to be composed of three senators, to be appointed by the president of the Senate, and three members of the House, to be appointed by the speaker thereof, shall provide for an examination to be held within ten days after the adoption of this resolution, to determine the qualifications of members, employés and correspondents.

Employés of the General Assembly who fail at such examination to recite correctly the Ten Commandments and the Golden Rule shall be dismissed, and newspaper correspondents who fail to pass such test shall be deprived of all floor privileges. Members failing in such test shall be deprived of all voting privileges until such disability is removed by passing a subsequent examination.

16

Public notice in the eminent *Republican-News* of Mt. Vernon:

WRONGFULLY ACCUSED

Having been accused of making and selling booze, will say no one has ever seen me drunk, or even drinking. And no one ever saw me make any attempt at making or selling booze, and I would like for the one who started that to prove it.

ARTHUR O'BANION

17

The Higher Learning at the Ohio State University, as described in its monthly bulletin:

Lectures will deal with ice cream formulas, ice cream testing, the handling of the raw cream, pasteurizing, standardizing, the preparation of mixes and the freezing of the same, the packing and preparing of the finished product for market. Attention will be given both to plain creams and fancy products, such as fruit and nut creams, pudding, lacto, etc. The subjects dealt with in lectures will be demonstrated by ample laboratory practice. The theory and practice of milk condensing will be given consideration under this subject.

18

Progress of Americanization among the slaves of the Cleveland Babbitts, as reported by the distinguished *Plain Dealer*:

Bill Dillinder, caddy master, has put caddying at the Westwood Country Club on a patriotic basis. A new flag-pole recently was erected in front of the clubhouse and each morning at 8 the flag is raised to the top with appropriate ceremonies by the youngsters. Lyman Fowles is captain and raises the flag while bugles are blown by Ferdinand Ransom and Donald Sautter and drums are beaten by Oscar Church and William Guger. After the flag is hoisted all the caddies sing " The Star Spangled Banner," " My Country 'Tis of Thee," or some other patriotic song.

19

Sporting offer of the Hon. Norman E. Tully, of Youngstown, O., in the esteemed *Vindicator* of that city for January 16 last:

I will lay a small wager that the long-looked-for Second Advent of Jesus will occur within five years.

20

Curious contribution to American history by the Rev. C. Jeffres McCombe, D.D., pastor of the Broad Street Methodist Episcopal Church of Columbus:

> Before going to Washington to take the oath of office the late President Harding said to Bishop William F. Anderson, of Cincinnati: "My prime motive in going to the White House is to bring America back to God."

21

The battle for virtue in the Anti-Saloon League region, as revealed by cuts ordered in a movie film, "Gambling Wives," by the Ohio Board of Censors:

> Cut out the sub-title, "As the night wore on the stakes grew larger, some hearts light, some hearts heavier," and substitute "As the night wore on, some hearts grew lighter and some hearts heavier."
>
> Cut out the sub-title, "Ann, don't you know that a man of his calibre doesn't make love to a girl like you?" and substitute "Ann, I don't like your going out this way."

22

The Higher Education at the Ohio State University, as described by the Columbus *Dispatch*:

> Wary Wade, a high ranking student at Ohio State, has the right angle on boxing. Every time out he is determined to learn something new, and he is making one beautiful effort to educate his already smart left hand. It is going to spell bad news for a lot of his future opponents. This boy trains daily and his improvement has been so remarkable that many of the

smart people in a boxing way predict a great future for
him. His clean-cut appearance is attracting attention
on the campus and groups of co-eds are becoming
unusually talkative.

23

Workings of the Holy Spirit in the domain of the Anti-
Saloon League, as described in a current press dispatch
from Columbus:

A letter received by Vernon M. Riegel, state director
of education, has been added to the "conscience
section" of his department. The letter is from a school
teacher who admits that during his service he has never
given the amount of time required by law to the teaching
of hygiene, thrift, and fire prevention. "I have written
this because I have promised God to make right everything in my life which is not or has not been right, as
near as possible," the letter says.

24

Printed card hanging in the bedrooms of a leading hotel
in the same city:

When entertaining guests of the opposite sex in one's
bedroom, it is customary to leave the door open at least
six inches.

OKLAHOMA

I

News note from the University of Oklahoma:

The new chapter of the Alpha Delta Sigma fraternity at the University is to be named after William Wrigley, Jr., the chewing gum manufacturer. Mr. Wrigley has promised to send the chapter his portrait, autographed and framed.

2

Uncompromising stand of R. A. Rooker, Democratic candidate for reëlection as alderman of Altus, as reported in the respectable *Times-Democrat* of the same city:

I am against Sunday baseball, mixed swimming pools, boys and girls petting parties and late hours auto riding. This may not lend to popularity, but I have not compromised on this question.

3

Contribution to the New Toxicology by the Muskogee correspondent of the Oklahoma City *News:*

Miss Allie Henderson, the Braggs school girl whom J. H. Davis, piano tuner, is alleged to have kidnaped October 21, took the witness stand here in the trial of Davis and testified that Davis gave her chewing gum that dazed her.

4

Editorial announcement in the *Baptist Messenger:*

We have just received a large shipment of baptismal pants. We can fit you and furnish your size without delay. Price, $22.50.

5

Sign over a popular restaurant in North Main Street, Oklahoma City:

EVERYONE OF OUR COOKS IS A MOTHER

6

From the platform of the Hon. S. R. Smith, a candidate for Congress in the Second Oklahoma District:

If any one commits a crime while he is under the influence, he must return the money or property or go to the pen and work it out at a reasonable wage before he serves his sentence for committing the crime.

If any one commits a crime while he is under the influence of intoxication he shall be punished double what he would be if he had done it while sober.

Any rancher or corporation must furnish bedding for the laborers when it is out of town. That would stop the blanket carrying in the West.

If any one has been found guilty of stealing or robbing without a doubt they can't get a pardon but must serve the sentence that is gave them.

No cold blooded murder should be allowed a pardon but should serve the sentence that is gave them.

No one should be allowed to gain their freedom by pleading the crazy act.

7

Optimistic note from the *Daily Oklahoman*, of Oklahoma City:

It will be at least another century before a second Woodrow Wilson is given to the people of America. Such supermen are not given to every generation.

8

From an optimistic sermon by the Rev. W. Clyde Howard, a favorite theologian of Oklahoma City:

Seventy years ago we were a nation of drinkers. Systematic work was begun all over America and the result has been the abolition of the drink evil and its utter overthrow. Please God, it shall never come back!

9

Mellow and uplifting outburst of the chief editorial writer of the *Daily Oklahoman*:

For all the church's pilgrims on this long and weary journey the Christ of the church has provided the means of grace, which are also the means of safety. There are the inspirations of public worship, the services of the sanctuary, the calm reflections of the holy Sabbath, the stimulating influence of the Sunday school, the call of charitable deeds, and the mighty strength to be derived from private devotion. All these and other means of grace have been provided that the pilgrim might not be exhausted and die on the long road that leads from the slough of despond to the delectable mountains.

10

Oklahoma's contribution to the roster of new crimes, as reported in a news dispatch from Okmulgee:

> Charged with "walking down the street with a questionable woman" T. H. Harvey, an oilfield worker, was arrested here and fined $10. Harvey met the girl, whom he said was an old friend, outside a moving-picture house and was walking down the street with her when arrested.

11

Dispatch from the fair town of Hobart, under the heading, " O. U. Boys Win Glory," in the celebrated Oklahoma City *News:*

> Nine more of Oklahoma University's alumni have become successful jazz musicians. Carl A. Smelser and Hershel Nix, formerly of this city, have written home from Montreal, Canada, where they are playing with George Freeman's orchestra, and report that they have started what promises to be a most successful season, opening at the Venitian Gardens in Montreal. All nine members of Freeman's band are former students or graduates of Oklahoma University.

12

Incident of life in Ku Kluxia, as reported in a press dispatch from Wichita:

> Armed deputies guarded all highways in this section today in an effort to capture an unidentified tourist, reported speeding across country with the bodies of his murdered wife and child. According to Mrs. John Roy,

who operates a filling station here, a man, woman and two children alighted from their automobile to purchase gasoline. The couple quarreled and the man, presumably the woman's husband, opened fire, killing the woman and one of the children. He then snatched up the bodies, pitched them in the rear seat of the car and with the other little girl sped away.

13

Extract from the proceedings of the Legislature of Oklahoma:

CHAPTER 302

Senate Resolution No. 14—Sidney Smith

Whereas, Sidney Smith, the creator of the Gumps, is to be in Oklahoma City, attending the Automobile Show on February 26 and 27, and

Whereas, as a student of affairs of state, his ideas are of material weight to members of law-making bodies:

Now, Therefore, Be It Resolved by the Senate of the State of Oklahoma, that the said Sidney Smith be invited to attend the session of February 27, at three o'clock in the afternoon, and address this body.

14

Another:

CHAPTER 290

*Senate Resolution No. 2—Tribute to Senator
S. Morton Rutherford, Deceased*

Our lips are poor ministers of our hearts on this occasion; a deep emotion is circuited by a meager scope when tethered to the spoken word. *The pool of sorrow stored in the heart's deep well is not reached by the buckets we lower of human speech.* It were a profanation of the sweetest flower the soul can bloom, could we coin into language and give to common gaze that which only sorrow may see. . . .

OREGON

Effects of the cheap dispersion of human knowledge in Oregon, as reported in a dispatch from Medford:

> John M. Eisenhour, 23 years old, died last night at Sacred Heart Hospital as the result of a 35-day fast. Suffering from ill health and reading in a physical culture magazine that fasting would cure him, he forsook food. When the case was reported to the local Red Cross Tuesday he was removed to the hospital, but the food and care administered there came too late.

2

Proud boast of the Hon. George L. Baker, 32°, mayor of Portland:

> A check of the records of the municipal court will show a larger amount of fines collected in Portland during the past year for law violations than were collected by similar courts in Los Angeles or San Francisco, despite their larger population.

3

Scientific progress in Portland, as reported in the local papers:

> Plays, opera and even circus programs have been broadcast by radio. But the Order of Hoot Owls,

conducting regular meetings from station KGW here, claims to be the first lodge in the world to conduct its ritualistic work over the ether waves.

4

Juristic news from the eminent Portland *Telegram:*

S. B. Davis, a Lane farmer, who was arrested recently for trapping duck out of season, sent a letter to Federal Prosecutor Joseph Stearns, asking to be allowed to plead guilty by mail. He inclosed a check for $50 to cover the fine.

"That's all right," said Judge Wolverton. "I'll accept the plea by mail—and as long as he has sent a check for $50, that will be the fine this court will impose."

The usual fine is $10.

5

Field sports at the Oregon Interstate Fair at Pineville, as reported by the estimable *Central Oregonian:*

A novelty was introduced by A. G. Bach in the spitting contest promoted by a chewing tobacco firm. He induced a dozen local chewers to enter and records were made by Lyle Laughlin, 27 feet; Lee Merchant, 24 feet; and R. L. Ireland, 20 feet.

6

Evidence of a rise of interest in dramatic art in Portland, from the letter column of the estimable *Oregonian:*

To the Editor—In last week's play of the Forest Taylor

stock company, " Sweet Seventeen," what color sweater did Ann Berryman wear in the first act, pink or blue?

A Subscriber.

Answer—According to Miss Berryman her sweater was rose with a few white stripes at the border.

7

Tribute to a gifted exhorter by the eminent *Coos Bay Times* of Marshfield, Coos county:

In his sermon this evening, the Rev. A. B. McReynolds, the Texas evangelist, will picture the death of Ezell Stepp, who was hanged at McKinney, Texas, last Winter. The evangelist is able to paint word pictures so vividly that children in the congregation almost gasped for breath Wednesday evening when he described the death of a little girl that fell into a 60-foot well during his last meeting. In describing the hanging of Ezell Stepp, Rev. A. B. McReynolds has had women scream aloud when he comes to the dramatic climax where the sheriff springs the trap.

8

From an address before the Advertising Club of Portland by the Hon. George S. Fowler, advertising director of Colgate & Company:

I challenge you to find a boy with a clean mouth and a dirty heart. The boy who washes his teeth twice a day doesn't go wrong. He can't.

9

Exitus of an ancient legal maxim, as recorded in a dispatch from Portland:

Speaking before the District Attorneys' Association of Oregon here last night, Governor Walter M. Pierce declared time has modified the old adage that every man's home is his castle and sanctuary, and in the future Oregon homes must be kept in such condition that a visit from an inspector of the State Prohibition forces will be welcomed at any time.

"The laws and customs have changed vastly since first was announced the right and doctrine that every man's home was his castle and sanctuary," the governor said. "The law clearly makes it your duty as district attorneys to co-operate with the Prohibition commissioner. We claim the right to go into any place in the State at any time as secret agents and to discover, if possible, law violations."

PENNSYLVANIA

I

Patriotic jocosities along the Delaware river, as reported by the Philadelphia *Evening Bulletin:*

> Several members of the Chester Rotary Club left the meeting last night after a speaker had made several bitter attacks on the United States, and had praised the I.W.W. At the end of his speech he removed a set of false whiskers and revealed himself as C. E. Swayze, chairman of the educational committee of the American Legion. He then addressed the Rotarians on the perils of Socialism, and told what the American Legion was doing to protect the government from its enemies. He was brought to the hall by Chief of Police Vance, and was supposedly an arrested prisoner.

2

From a signed editorial by the publisher of the Altoona *Mirror* in the fiftieth anniversary issue of his estimable gazette:

> The one outstanding fact of the success the *Mirror* has attained has been primarily the faith in and accountability to God, our Heavenly Father, and the acknowledgment of the same.
> Business is religion.
> Religion is God.
> God is Truth.
> Many, many times have I heard the founder of the

Mirror, my beloved father, talk to his Heavenly Father about the *Mirror*. And here let me say to you business men and others: There is nothing that can take the place of prayer.

3

Progress of human knowledge in Erie, as reported by the eminent *Daily Times*:

The Rev. Dr. Brownlee said that when the devil was thrown out of heaven, he took a great hoſt of angels with him, and they have become demons and allies of the devil, and much sickness is due to the faƈt that these demons get into folks and produce all kinds of trouble. The only way to cure this kind of sickness is to caſt out the demons. " I have seen patients cured of fits in a very few seconds," he said.

4

Progress of Chriſtian thought in Philadelphia, as reported by the *Public Ledger*:

Proteſting because the moſt popular piƈture at the Academy of the Fine Arts exhibition, as decided by vote, for the third time was a nude, the Rev. G. E. Nichols, paſtor of the Firſt Baptiſt Church, Seventeenth above Walnut ſtreet, asks that in the future there be a conteſt to decide the moſt liked painting, excluding nudes.

" Does it not seem unfortunate that the moſt popular piƈture decided by popular vote, at the exhibition recently closed at the Academy of the Fine Arts should again be a nude? " he asks. " It is the third time that the choice of the public has been given to that subjeƈt. Might it not be well the coming year to make the conteſt one among the other piƈtures put on exhibition, excluding the nude? "

5

Ideal of Service behind the recent military Vice Crusade in Philadelphia, as reported by the war correspondent of the Scripps-Howard newspapers:

Philadelphia politicians ask why Mayor Kendrick put his head into this sort of a moral noose. The best answer they can give themselves is that he is looking beyond Philadelphia toward the governor's chair in Harrisburg and is willing to ditch the organization for the time being to win the rest of the State. Another and less flattering theory propounded out of the corners of their mouths is the suggestion that, after all, the inside organization men can sacrifice the perquisites of the police department so long as other departments are not interfered with. They have in mind Philadelphia's big construction program, running into many millions of dollars.

6

Dispatch from Harrisburg:

A patriotic doctor who objected to placards bearing the warning " German measles " was notified today by Dr. J. M. Campbell, chief of the Bureau of Communicable Diseases of the State Health Department, that the phraseology of the warning cards cannot be changed. The patriotic doctor suggested that " victory " or " liberty " measles be substituted for " German."

7

Theologico-judicial dictum of the Rev. W. E. P. Haas, pastor of Wharton Memorial M. E. Church, Philadelphia:

A piece of ice on the doorstep of a Christian home on Sunday is a disobedience to God.

8

Intellectual recreation of a stalwart American of the proud town of Berwick, as reported by the Philadelphia *Record:*

A. B. Lynn, who last year counted more than 200,000 automobiles passing his home, has resumed counting. . . . Wednesday evenings and Sunday afternoons and evenings he devotes to the task. Last year he counted the first 100,000 machines in 251 hours, and the second 100,000 in 215 hours, all on Sunday and Wednesday evenings.

9

Incautious *obiter dictum* of the editor of *Serving and Waiting*, the organ of the Philadelphia School of the Bible, 1721-25 Spring Garden Street:

A religion in which all men agree is anything but the Christian religion.

10

Contribution to theological science by a learned reader of the eminent Gettysburg *Times:*

To the Editor of the Times:
Sir: The basis of calculations of the size of Heaven is found in Revelation XXXI, 16: " And he measured the city with the reed, 12,000 furlongs. The length and the breadth and the height of it are equal."

Twelve thousand furlongs are 7,920,000 feet, or 1,500 miles. The cube of this must be taken in order to obtain the total dimensions of Heaven, which are 469,793,088,000,000,000,000,000 cubic feet.

With these figures before us, we can figure out just how much room there is in Heaven for each individual soul. A single calculation is given to prove just how easy the process really is. The meeting place of the angels probably is the most spacious and requires at least half the total space. We deduct another fourth for streets and open places, which leaves 124,198,272,000,-000,000,000 cubic feet for the actual dwelling place of the angels.

A room twenty feet square contains 8,000 cubic feet. Assuming that the dwellings of Heaven are divided into rooms of twenty feet square, there would be exactly 13,024,534,000,000,000 rooms. The present number of inhabitants of the world is estimated at approximately 1,000,000,000. Assuming for the moment that this number has always existed in the world each day and that there are three generations in a century, the number of inhabitants for each century would be 3,000,000,000.

Assuming also that the world has existed for 1,000 centuries (scientists have not been able to agree as to the age of the earth), then the total number of inhabitants in the world amounts to 3,000,000,000,000.

Many scientists are of the opinion that other worlds besides the earth, especially Mars, are inhabited. Not to leave out of account the possible inhabitants of other worlds, it is estimated that ninety-nine of them could be added, giving a total of one hundred worlds like the earth with 300,000,000,000,000 inhabitants. Dividing the total number of rooms, 13,024,534,000,000,000, by 300,000,000,000,000, the total number of inhabitants, there would be nearly five rooms, twenty feet square and with a twenty-foot ceiling, for each angel.

E. L. WEIKERT, JR.

11

The strenuous life on the western frontiers of Pennsylvania, as reported by the Beaver Falls *Tribune:*

Monday forenoon fire broke out at the Dam school, Big Beaver township. The fire alarm was given by the school, those hearing first call quickly organized and selected S. A. Duncan fire chief, W. G. McHattie and Norman McHattie, firemen; Wayne Duncan driver of the chemical truck and Wayne McHattie driver of the hook and ladder truck. After organization the company immediately proceeded to the scene of the fire. After preparing the chemicals and placing the ladders the chief went in search of the blaze, but the teacher informed him that she, with the help of her pupils, had extinguished the fire some time during the early part of the day. The teacher thanked the company for their prompt response and invited them to remain and visit the school.

12

Footnote on Law Enforcement from the columns of the illustrious Philadelphia *Record:*

A few days ago a new face appeared at roll-call of the Prohibition force in the office of Divisional Chief Ruben B. Sams, 1913 Arch street. After roll-call the new dry sleuth stepped upon a little box in the room and said, " Gentlemen, let us pray." The agents, thinking that a joke was being sprung on them, started to laugh. . . .

13

From the church news of the late *North American:*

Baptisms with a spotlight playing upon minister and candidates as they stand in the pool will take place tomorrow evening in the Fifth Baptist Church, Eighteenth and Spring Garden streets. The Rev. Dr. George W. Swope has introduced the spotlight innovation in connection with extensive improvements, costing $20,000, made on the church. The baptistry has been enlarged, and when Doctor Swope and a candidate enter the pool a white spotlight will play upon them in the darkened church. As the candidate is immersed the color will change to purple.

14

From a report of an address by the Hon. Joseph A. Turner, of Roanoke, Va., before the Philadelphia Rotary Club:

He quoted an English Rotarian as saying that Rotary was more than a luncheon club; it was a posture of the soul.

15

Counter offensive against the Pope in Chester county, as revealed by the distinguished West Chester *Daily Local News:*

Milk from a Holstein cow; Protestants only. Reba Marie Jacons, New Centreville.

16

Advance information from the Rev Dr. George Edward Hawes, a favorite divine of Harrisburg, as reported in the celebrated *Evening News* of that city:

Heaven is a city 15,000 miles square or 6,000 miles around. One side is 245 miles longer than the entire

length of the Great Walls of China. Walls surrounding
Heaven are 396,000 times higher than the Great Wall
of China and eight times as thick. Heaven has twelve
gates, three on each side and has room for 100,000,-
000,000 souls. There are no slums. The entire city
is built of diamond material, and the streets are paved
with gold. All inhabitants are honest and there are no
locks, no courts and no policemen.

17

Law Enforcement news from the up-and-coming town of
Scranton:

Three local saloons are to be placed on the black list
of the local bartenders' union unless they employ union
bartenders. This was the decision reached at a meeting
of the Central Labor Union. The saloon business is so
prosperous in Scranton that the bartenders' union is
planning to demand higher wages.

18

Amendment of the First Amendment in Pennsylvania,
as reported in a dispatch from Wilkes-Barre:

Mayor Daniel L. Hart today supported the action of
members of the American Legion in breaking up a
meeting called to honor the name and memory of
Nicholai Lenin. To members of the Workers' Party of
America, who protested that their right of free speech
had been abrogated, he declared that in the future the
city will not issue a license for any public meeting *unless
such a meeting is approved by the American Legion.*

19

From a communication by the Hon. William B. Yeakel, of Coopersburg, Pa., in the *Farm Journal:*

Mr. William S. Hallman wants to know if life insurance is a good inveſtment. I say, absolutely no! In what way is it right for a man, made in the image of God, to walk around with a price on his head, payable after death?

20

From the circular of a Harrisburg firm:

SELECT ANY TEN SPEECHES FOR ONLY $3.00

The speeches liſted below run 1000 words each and are suitable for use at Fraternal Societies, Lodges, Clubs, Debating Classes, Political meetings and Luncheon Clubs. We will sell you any 5 speeches for $2.00, any 10 speeches for $3.00, any 15 for $4.00 or any 20 for $5.00. What speeches do you want?

Rotary, the Applied Science of Living.

The Hiſtory, Purpose, Accomplishments and Recent Statiſtics of the Benevolent and Protective Order of Elks.

Address to be Given before the Grand Lodge of the Knights of Pythias and the Grand Courts of Calanthe.

Speech to be used in Visiting Lodges of the Independent Order of B'rith Abraham.

Address at Reception to the State Commander of the American Legion.

Speech of Newly Elected Senior Warden in Masonic Blue Lodge.

Address at Banquet to Retiring Paſtor of Lutheran Church.

The Influence of Highway Transportation upon Religious Life.

Speech at the Presentation of an Automobile to a Pastor.
Address to be Delivered by the President of a Jewish Sisterhood.
A Letter of Condolence on the Death of a Member of an Eastern Star Chapter.
A Short Talk by a New Member when Admitted to the Ladies' Rotary Club.
Address of Welcome at Second Anniversary of the Daughters of America.
Address at Banquet of Coal Miners' Club.
Speech at Complimentary Dinner to Winner of a Golf Championship.
The Need of More Business for Negroes.

21

The burdens of life in the remoter fastnesses of Lancaster county, as revealed by a letter to the editor of the eminent Lancaster *New Era:*

The citizens of Lincoln wish to appeal to your journal for help in a situation that is rapidly becoming intolerable. We are again infested with skunks.

22

From an article by Clarence Budington Kelland in the world-famous *Saturday Evening Post:*

Who shall say, when mundane affairs are put to the last analysis, when they are sent to the ultimate laboratory for assay, that a perfect sawmill, a perfect real-estate sale, a perfect grocery store, will not show to the Great Chemist as high in gold as the perfect painting, the perfect sonata or the perfect sculpture? Who may claim that a higher ability goes to the creating of one than the other?

23

Effects of the missionary work of Dr. Stokowsky and his orchestra in Philadelphia, as reported by the eminent *Inquirer*:

> Mayor Kendrick was presented with a gold harmonica last night at the Metropolitan Opera House. . . . " Play something! " commanded a voice from the audience. The Mayor played " Barney Google " and an Irish reel. " With this beautiful harmonica I am going to practice all through the year," he said, " and next year I'll be able to do much better."

24

Dictum of the Rev. Peter H. Hershey, chaplain of Post No. 27 of the American Legion, as reported by the estimable Harrisburg *Evening News:*

> If you tear the Eighteenth Amendment out of the Constitution you might as well tear one of the stripes out of our flag.

25

Contribution to theology by the Society of The First Division, in its history of the same, published in the Quaker metropolis of Philadelphia:

> War is indeed a holy thing, and they who experience its purging and its exaltation exemplify those divine attributes which the Maker gave when He created man in His own image. A soldier expressed this truth when he said to his chaplain, " In battle we are all chaplains."

RHODE ISLAND

I

Progress of the Higher Learning at Brown University, as reported by the *New Student*:

> At Brown a Junior Kiwanis Club is being organized. The organization will include " men on the campus interested in boosting the name of Brown."

SOUTH CAROLINA

I

A Blackville dispatch to the Columbia papers:

One of the most unique, unusual and important events of the season occurred here Tuesday evening, when Miss Martha Abigail Sanders and Mr. Ulysses Sill were united in marriage in the Baptist church. The symbols and color scheme of the Ku Klux Klan made beautiful decorations. The lights of the church were turned out, and the fiery cross, illuminated by many tiny electric lights, threw a lovely glow over the scene. It is estimated that there were 1,100 people present; 300 could not be seated. Promptly at 8 o'clock the wedding march began. Preceding the bridal party Klansmen began to march down both aisles, single file, turning near the rostrum and lining themselves against both side walls of the large auditorium, the lines almost filling both walls of the building. Next came the bridal party, consisting of eight Klansmen and eight bridesmaids. The bride, who was never more lovely than in the robe of the order, carrying a beautiful bouquet of bride roses, entered with the dame of honor. They were met on the rostrum by the groom and the officiating minister, a Klansman. All who took part in the wedding were robed, and all were masked except the bride and groom and dame of honor.

2

Opinion of the Rev. Dr. Billy Sunday credited to the Hon. William D. Melton, LL.B., LL.D., president of the University of South Carolina, chairman of the South Carolina Four-Minute Men during the World War, author of " Our Country: Its Foundations, Its Problems and Its Future," and member of the American Bar Association, the Kappa Sigma fraternity, and the Ancient Arabic Order of Nobles of the Mystic Shrine:

I believe him to be the world's greatest evangelist, and long to hear him again.

3

From a circular sent to members of Congress by the go-getting sales manager of the Saroco Laboratories, Union, S.C.:

Gentlemen of Congress, we sympathize with you; yours is a difficult task. Instead of pouring oil on troubled waters, you are to take troubled oil out of the waters.

For weeks now the Ship of State has been rocking from the tempest in a Teapot Dome. Yours is the task to take the " dough " from Doheny, examine the " sin " in Sinclair, and investigate what the " clean " in McLean means.

Our is a different mission. While you are washing Washington clear of oil scandal, allow us to suggest to you a capital dome-cleanser for every " coco " beneath the Capitol Dome. Not only do we need clean hands, but a clean scalp. We have a Sham Poo that is real; it will meet your vital needs. Cocoa Oil for coco nuts.

Remember, that when Samson lost his hair, he lost

his strength; Caroco will help you avoid his fate. It is made in Union (S.C.) for all the Union.

Gentlemen of Congress, your mental activity withers your hair roots; we offer you the antidote.

4

From a call for 33,373 volunteers to teach the 33,373 white adult illiterates of the State how to write their names:

Just a few days ago a man said in our presence that a strong, vigorous man had come to him very much exercised about his spiritual welfare. He was at once referred to certain passages in the Bible, which would unquestionably throw light upon his perplexity. This strong, vigorous man was forced to reply: " I am very sorry, but I cannot read."

We wonder whether any other argument is really necessary to make the people of this State determine to remove adult illiteracy, thus putting it within the power of every white man and woman in this State of ours to search the Scriptures and thus learn of Him, whom to know aright is life everlasting.

5

Additional inducement:

A revised copy of Æsop's Fables will be given by Mr. Ambrose E. Gonzalez to each pupil who learns to write his name.

6

Progress of Baptist theology among the Tar Heels, as reported by the intelligent Columbia *State:*

Denial of State appropriations to any institution permitting the teaching of the theory that man sprang from a monkey or ape will be proposed in an evolution bill to be introduced by Senator George W. Wightman, of Saluda. In another bill Senator Wightman will provide for the expulsion from State educational institutions of any teacher, professor or officer who denies the divinity of Christ.

7

Lamentable doctrinal differences among the total immersionists along the Waccamaw river, as revealed by a letter to the editor of the estimable *Horry Herald*, of Conway:

I beg space in your paper in reply to an article concerning the trouble between Pete McCracken and his wife.

I do not know the author of the article, but it seems that the blame was placed on the Second Baptist church for its influence over Pete's wife. I beg to say that the Second Baptist church has tried to use its influence for good. I also wish to say that Mrs. McCracken has never applied to the Second Baptist church for membership, but did join the First Baptist church of Conway, and the trouble arose because Pete didn't want Mrs. McCracken baptized in the pool of the First Baptist church of Conway, but believed in the example set by Christ who was baptized in the river Jordan,—that she should go to the river.

Yours respectfully,
ED. G. NORMAN,
Clerk Second Baptist Church.

8

Trials of the Fundamentalists, as revealed by a letter to the *Baptist Courier*, the leading organ of Christian thought between the Peedee and Tugaloo rivers:

> The South Main Street Church of Greenwood is again without a pastor. It came in such a short time after we had gone through with the trials of securing one to whom the church was devoted and whom it had hoped to keep for years, but it seems that it had to be; for that Earle Street, Greenville, crowd just kept working until they got us in this fix. Personally, I have no censure for any one of them, because I must love my brethren, but they had better mind, and keep away from Greenwood the remainder of their days. Trying to locate a pastor is no little job. Our prayer is for a message from heaven, naming the man upon whom the Lord has laid his hands to do this blessed work.

9

From the platform of the Hon. Mountain Lion Sloan, a candidate for public office in Greenville county:

> I believe in outlawing liquor because it's bad and I believe in outlawing swimming-pools because they're bad. I'm against them, and I'm going to do all I can to put them out of business. How a man could let his wife go to one with a crowd in which there are other men, and still live with her, is more than I can see.

10

Theologico-ethical inquiry received by the Bible Editor of the Greenville *News*, and printed by him in that great newspaper:

Q.—I have been a widow for over a year now,—for exactly sixteen months next week. I was married to my first husband only about three years. Long before his death we had grown tired of each other, and had confessed it to each other. Now a real love comes into my life. I know, of course, that not much time will have to elapse before I could marry without being condemned as too hasty by even the most eager to find fault. But I am wondering if the Bible says anything about this? I wish you would send me the references. And I would like also to have references on the subject sent in by your readers, if they will be so kind as to write to me.

Mrs. X.Z.X.L.

A.—All references mailed. All letters gladly forwarded.

11

Supernatural events along the Waccamaw river, as described in the vernacular prints of those parts:

While Edmund Bigham was being tried for murder at Conway recently, George Steele, a witness, died in the witness chair from a sudden attack of heart disease. Shortly after Judge Rice had sentenced Bigham to be electrocuted, after the jury found him guilty of murder without recommendation, the judge went to Florence to hold court, and the evening before court opened, while he was sitting in a theater, he was stricken with some eye affliction which prevented him from presiding the next morning.

According to the Florence *Times*, when it was announced that the judge was incapacitated from holding court, expressions were heard from persons to the effect that the " Bigham curse " was manifesting itself, and that " they had better turn Edmund Bigham loose, or he will cause the death of many others! " This paper also recalls that when Bigham was first tried and convicted of exterminating the Bigham family at Florence, three years ago, the day was bright and sunny, but just after the verdict of guilty without recommendation had been brought in, " within three minutes a perfect gale was blowing, and one of the worst wind and rain storms seen in Florence in a long time raged for a few minutes."

The Horry *Herald*, published at Conway, says that the night of the day that the Colleton county jury brought in its verdict of guilty in the Bigham case, " according to the testimony of several reliable Conwayites, there was a distinct earthquake shock felt in that town."

12

Short view of the rewards vouchsafed to consecrated men among the Fundamentalists:

Please give me space in your paper to thank my good people for their kind deeds. At Thanksgiving, Crossroads and Thompson Creek churches gave us two good poundings, filling our pantry with all kinds of good things to eat, then Providence came in with a new leather valise and a Stetson hat. Then at Christmas Ruby dressed me up with a new suit of clothes and shoes. Then, better still, all four of these churches presented me with a new Ford car the night before Christmas. I want to thank every one who helped to do this and ask the prayers of all that I may be a faithful pastor and render such service as will honor God and be a blessing to my fellow man.

J. D. Purvis.

Ruby, S.C.

13

The delicate ebb and flow of race prejudice among the Nordic blonds of the South Carolina Legislature, as reported by the Greenville *Piedmont:*

When the colored president of the Colored Normal, Industrial, Agricultural and Mechanical College, a State Institution, appeared before a committee of the Legislature last year, he wore a suit that had evidently been made by expert tailors. This fact stirred an unexpressed prejudice against him in the mind of the legislators, but it was quickly removed when he told them that the suit had been fashioned by students of his college who were learning the tailoring trade.

SOUTH DAKOTA

I

The development of ecclesiastical ranks and dignities in the former haunts of the buffalo and the coyote, as revealed by the signatures to a petition presented to Congress by the Federation Council of the Churches of Christ in South Dakota:

THE REV. DAVIS J. PERRIN, D.D.
First Vice Superintendent of the Congregational Churches of South Dakota.

THE REV. A. PIERCE WALTZ
Second Vice Pastor of the Baptist Church at Ipswich, S. Dak.

THE REV. G. E. BOHNER
Third Vice Superintendent of the Evangelical Churches of South Dakota.

THE REV. D. M. BUTT
Fourth Vice Retired Former Superintendent of the Aberdeen District of the Presbyterian Church.

2

Progress of art on the steppes, as revealed by the eminent Yankton *Press:*

Legislators gathering here have received word that a representative of the National Association for the

Improvement of the Appearance of Hogs will urge that the appearance of swine should be uniform and artistic.

3

Communication received by a Sioux Falls newspaper from a subscriber in Garretson:

I have taken your paper for twenty-four years and hitherto have found no fault with it. When you began running cross-word puzzles they were very good and possible to work, but lately they have been harder and now are almost impossible to solve. Having written you about this matter and received no satisfaction, I am compelled to abandon your good newspaper and take another which prints puzzles which can be worked without staying up all night.

4

Enforcing the First Amendment to the Constitution in South Dakota, as described in a dispatch from Sturgis:

The Board of Education at Faith, S.D., has authority to expel high school students who leave the school while the Bible is being read, Judge James McNenny ruled today in the case of A. Finger vs. the School Board. The mandamus proceedings were brought by the plaintiff, who represented Catholics at Faith, to force the School Board to reinstate students who had been dismissed because they refused to remain in the classroom during the Bible reading.

5

Extract from a bill recently introduced in the State legislature by the Hon. Gladys Pyle:

HOUSE BILL NO. 84

Section 10023. *Allowance by County.*—For the partial support of any woman whose husband is dead . . . or any woman who has been divorced from her husband in this State for a period of one year or more, when such woman is pregnant . . .

TENNESSEE

I

From a discourse by the Rev. Dr. Billy Sunday to the gaping Christians of Nashville, as reported by the celebrated *Banner:*

Our country is filled with a Socialistic, I.W.W., communistic, radical, lawless, anti-American, anti-church, anti-God, anti-marriage gang, and they are laying the eggs of rebellion and unrest in labor and capital and home; and we have some of them in the universities. I can take you through the universities and pick out a lot of black-hearted communistic fellows who are teaching that to the boys and sending them out to undermine America. If this radical element could have their way, my friends, the laws of nature would be repealed, or they would reverse them; oil and water would mix; the turtle dove would marry the turkey buzzard; the sun would rise in the West and set in the East; chickens would give milk and cows would lay eggs; the pigs would crow and the roosters would squeal; cats would bark and dogs would mew; the least would be the greatest; a part would be greater than the whole; yesterday would be day after tomorrow if that crowd were in control.

2

Progress of the New Jurisprudence, as reported by a news dispatch from Chattanooga:

> M. B. Partain, a farmer, was awarded $2 damages in the Circuit Court here today against R. B. Alexander, a subscription solicitor for the Chattanooga *Times*, for " mental anguish, worry and loss of sleep " caused by his failure to receive the paper after he had subscribed for it.

3

From a public bull by the Hon. Noah W. Cooper, an eminent Nashville jurisconsult and candidate for the United States Senate:

> Repealing the Sunday closing law will be a step toward Hell. Just think of Nashville opening up her gasoline stations on Sunday! The Devil has no quicker way to ruin than the Sabbath-breaking way. It hurries up to Hell. Hundreds of cities have been ruined by Sabbath-breaking.

4

Press dispatch from Nashville, in the heart of Fundamentaldom:

> Claiming to own the stone with which David slew Goliath, R. M. Johnson, of Morristown, has asked Wilbur Nelson, State geologist, to inspect and value it. He said the stone had been in his family since Biblical times.

5

Ecclesiastical notice appearing on all the lamp-posts and dead walls of Knoxville:

HAPPY SUNDAY EVENINGS
At Church Street Methodist Episcopal Church
Dr. Knickerbocker will preach on
BEES AND BUTTERFLIES,
giving a funeral oration on a dead butterfly.

6

The rise of literary passion in Knoxville, as described by the gifted *Journal:*

" The Novel as an Interpretation of Life " was the subject of an exceedingly interesting address by Mrs. J. K. Harold before the Knoxville branch of the League of American Penwomen Thursday afternoon. . . . Each member gave the title of some novel which had made a deep impression on her at some time. Dickens seems the favorite author of the league, with Gene Stratton-Porter as the favorite modern novelist.

7

The process of Law Enforcement in the great Christian city of Bristol, as described in the eminent *News* by the Rev. Dr. George F. Robertson:

Let everybody of any race or color who knows or has heard of any violations of any law in Bristol write the same to the president of the Good Citizenship Club, 1030 Windsor avenue, and say so. If it is only hearsay, so state it. . . . If you do not care to be known, your request for secrecy will be kept to the very letter. No one will in any way be compromised.

8

Ecclesiastical amenities in the Baptist Holy Land, as reported in a press dispatch from Chattanooga:

Cordial relations have been restored between Evangelist Gipsy Smith and the Rev. W. B. Rutledge, North Chattanooga pastor, who was taken to task Wednesday evening for being asleep at Dr. Smith's revival service. At the noonday meeting yesterday, after Dr. James I. Vance of Nashville had offered prayer, the evangelist said he desired to say a word about the incident of the previous night. He said he did not know the sleeper was a minister and expressed deep regret that he had hurt anybody. " I would rather hurt myself," he said. At this point the Rev. Wm. Rutledge stepped into the pulpit and shook hands with the evangelist, as the choir and audience sang " Praise God From Whom All Blessings Flow."

TEXAS

Perils of club life in El Paso, as described by the alert *Herald* of that great city:

Her raid on the Elks' Club Sunday night, when she claimed she found her husband and other men playing cards for money, was detailed by Mrs. Hinden Butler to the members of the El Paso Federation of Women's Clubs at its meeting in the Hotel Paso del Norte. Mrs. Butler is the president of the organization and she did not mince words in describing her visit to the club.

" When my daughter and I entered the office of the Elks' Club Sunday night, the room was empty," Mrs. Butler said. " I crossed the billiard room towards the card room, and met Ben Stein, the manager. He greeted me, and told me he would see if he could find Mr. Butler. He started for the card room, but I beat him to it.

" Around a large table there sat 10 or 12 men. They were playing poker. In front of my husband was a pile of money. Several other games were in progress, but I was particularly concerned with the game where money was being used.

" I recognized two of the men playing with Mr. Butler, and my daughter pointed out a third whose name she knew. I am in possession of the names of these men, and I mean to swear out warrants for all four, including my husband."

2

Rise of moral delicacy among Texas dog-fanciers, as revealed by an advertisement in the El Paso papers:

Legitimate Chihuahua pups for sale cheap.

3

Application of theology to scientific salesmanship among the Texas Baptists, as reported by the Dallas *Times-Herald*:

More than 100 men attended the opening lecture of the Y.M.C.A. salesmanship course in the Y.M.C.A. auditorium Wednesday evening, marking the beginning of a sixteen-week session given by the Dallas Institute of Technology School of Commerce. Frank Moran, addressing the group on "Salesmanship as a Profession," mentioned that salesmanship dated back to Biblical times. Among other things he said that Christ Himself sold Christianity to His disciples and His disciples sold it to others, and that it had been so well sold that nobody else had ever been able to sell any other form of religion.

4

From the code of regulations for the Woman's Building at the University of Texas:

The young ladies will be expected to consult invariably with the Director before making arrangements for going to entertainments or places of recreation; to regulate their conduct according to her decision, and to return promptly after night entertainments. Sitting on the steps or lingering about the door with escorts will be considered a violation of propriety.

In conformity with the expressed wish of the Board of Regents, gentlemen visitors can be received on the first floor only.

Each young lady is requested to procure for her bedroom windows sash curtains, which must be kept down at all times. At night, as long as the room lights are burning, the blinds must be down and closed.

Negligée costumes must not be worn on the first floor at any time.

5

Follow-up letter employed upon ungrateful patients by a medical man of Paige, Texas:

NOTICE

I expect a prompt settlement of all accounts due me.

If not possible to settle in cash, any of the following named articles will be acceptable, viz.:

Cotton Seed, Chickens, Ducks, Geese, Turkeys, Billy Goats, Live Cat Fish over 1 lb. each, Bull Dogs, Registered Bird Dogs, Live Wild Cats, Poland China Hogs, Skunk Hides (dry), Deer Hides, Shot Guns, Cedar Posts, Watches, Gold Teeth, Diamonds, Cream Checks, Pine Trees (2 ft. in diameter x 30 ft. long), Automobiles new or second hand, Peanuts, Black Eyed Peas, Liberty Bonds, Land Notes, Bacon, Lard, Country Hams, Clean Goose Feathers, Soft Shell Turtles over 5 lbs. each. Anything that can be sold for cash legally.

I need the money.

6

Troubles of the learned in the Bible Belt, as reported in a dispatch from Waco:

Because he did not believe that Noah's ark, with the dimensions mentioned in the Bible, was capable of accommodating a pair of all the animals extant in the world at Noah's time and because he had been criticized for expressing that belief, C. S. Fothergill, instructor in history at Baylor university, resigned today.

7

The rewards of a gifted pastor in the Trinity river bottom-lands, as reported by the distinguished Fort Worth *Record*:

The Rev. Weeping Wayne Allison, known in Southern Baptist circles as the Broken-Hearted Disciple because of his spirituality, is honored and esteemed in his sphere in much the same manner that Walter Johnson, the grand old man of baseball, is regarded by the baseball public of America.

8

Public bull by the Hon. R. C. Johnston, mayor of the beautiful and up-and-coming city of Waxahachie:

A WARNING TO BOYS

We are being worried a great deal with complaints about donkeys running at large in the city. They walk about on the lawns and worry the people and I do not blame them for complaining. And now, boys, we want to warn you to not let your donkies loose to worry people, but keep them up and enjoy them. It is unlawful for them to run at large and we insist on enforcing this law. We are not quarreling at you, we want you to have your pets, but please see that they do not bother other people. Boys, always remember to do unto others as you would have them do unto you.

Thank you, boys,

R. C. Johnston, *Mayor*

9

Effects of Christian preaching in Dallas, as reported by the estimable *News*:

> An employé of one of the largest bookshops in Texas recently managed to get hold of a copy of an obscene book, paying about $5 for it. He offered it to a prominent business man in one of the prominent towns of Texas, and the man immediately paid $20 for it.

10

Novel contribution to the American language by Texas Baptists, as revealed by news notes in the *Baptist Standard* of Dallas:

> Work starts well on the Carlton-Olin field. Within the last three weeks a brand-new six-room *pastorium* has been built, insured for three years, pastor's family moved in and graciously pounded, and salary paid to the end of the year.
>
> Dr. McHenry Seal is leading the San Saba Church in a beautiful way. The spiritual life of the church is good in spite of the fact that it has just built an excellent *pastorium* and a two-story annex to the church building.

11

Progress of Fundamentalist jurisprudence in the great republic of Texas, as reported by the National Association for the Advancement of Colored Peoples:

> At Bishop, Texas, one Smith, a colored physician, was burned to death after his hands and feet had been

cut off. It was alleged that Dr. Smith, while riding in his automobile, collided with a car occupied by whites.

12

From a circular distributed by Nordic Blond evangelists at a recent revival in Dallas under the leadership of the Rev. Dr. Bob Jones, an eminent pastor of those remote steppes:

> I am a Searchlight on a high tower.
>
> I run my relentless eye to and fro throughout the land; my piercing glance penetrates the brooding places of Iniquity. I plant my eyes and ears in the whispering Corridors of Crime.
>
> Wherever men gather furtively together, there am I, an austere and invisible Presence. I am the Recording Angel's Proxy.
>
> When I invade the fetid dens of Infamy there is a sudden scampering and squeaking as of rats forsaking a doomed ship.
>
> I am the haunting dread of the depraved and the hated Nemesis of the vicious.
>
> The foe of Vice, the friend of Innocence, the rod and staff of Law, I am—
>
> THE KU KLUX KLAN.

13

Sweetly solemn thought by the editor of the eminent *News* of Dallas:

> If Carnegie medals were awarded for the endurance of pain and suffering alone, many a sick, weak woman who suffers from so-called female troubles would be entitled to the highest honors.

14

Program of the World's Fundamentalist Convention at Fort Worth, as reported to the *Christian Century* by the Rev. Dr. C. D. Meade:

1. The withdrawal of financial and moral support from all church schools that teach any theory of evolution whatsoever.

2. The immediate revision of all text-books that teach any theory of evolution whatsoever.

3. Compulsory measures to force all teachers to sign annually a statement of creed which affirms a firm and steadfast faith in the Genesis account of creation, the historical fact of all Bible miracles, the virgin birth, the bodily resurrection, the imminent second coming of Jesus, the existence of a personal devil and a literal hell.

4. Political and financial pressure brought to bear upon all tax-supported schools in order to eliminate both textbooks and instructors teaching any form of evolution whatsoever.

5. The rejection of the uniform interdenominational Sunday-school lessons because of their evolutionary and post-millennial tendencies.

6. The compulsory resignation of all pastors, evangelists and Sunday-school teachers who hold to any theory of evolution whatsoever.

7. The organization of a Fundamentalist Society within each local church for the purpose of propaganda.

8. Wherever denominational church schools do not fall in line with the Fundamentalist demands on Bible interpretation and elimination of the teaching of evolutionary theories, the Fundamentalists will organize, finance and give moral support to Bible schools that will give instruction in Bible and science in harmony with Fundamentalists' beliefs.

15

Proof that scientific research is not stopped by the triumph of Fundamentalism, from a dispatch from Canyon, in the Baptist he-man belt:

The net material value of an average human being is 98 cents, according to analytical research made by Dr. C. A. Pierle, head of the department of chemistry in West Texas Teachers' College.

Dr. Pierle has found the body of a man weighing 150 pounds, if divided into its component chemical elements, would contain enough water to wash a pair of blankets, enough iron to make a ten-penny nail, enough lime to whitewash a small chicken coop and enough sulphur to kill the fleas on a good-sized dog. All these elements, he estimates, could be purchased at a drug store for 98 cents.

16

From the last will and testament of a loyal citizen of the Invisible Empire:

When these ears no longer hear the tender voice of loved ones, and these eyes are closed in that ever dreamless sleep; when these feet no longer tread this mundane sphere, and these hands are folded upon a motionless breast; when this tongue is paralyzed and forever still, and these lips no longer move at the impulse of my will; when this old body has become a lump of lifeless clay to be consigned back to mother earth; and this spirit has taken its farewell flight to worlds unknown; when my heart-broken loved ones gaze upon my motionless form through tear-dimmed eyes, and my friends stand by with sad faces and heavy hearts; in that mysterious sleep of death, I ask for no greater honor and no more glorious tribute than to have my cold, pulseless frame wrapped in the sacred folds of a Klansman's robe, my gray, unconscious head covered with a Klansman's helmet with the visor folded back so the passers-by may look upon my unresponsive face; to have white-robed Klansmen bear me to the open grave, lower my casket into the tomb and fill the yawning chasm with tender loving hands.

I ask for no profusion of flowers or elaborate floral offerings; but just a simple Fiery Cross in blood-red roses, inscribed with the mystic letters K.K.K. in flowers of purest white. For a tombstone to mark my resting place, I ask no expensive sepulchre, or costly shaft of marble—just a simple granite slab, cut with the hands of Klansmen good and true, from the top of Stone Mountain, in Georgia, where the Knights of the Ku Klux Klan had its origin on that memorable Thanksgiving night in 1915.

I ask for no greater tribute of honor and respect and no more glorious recommendation to generations yet unborn, than to have chiseled thereon these simple but sublime words:

"HERE LIES A KLANSMAN."

And as the ceaseless ages roll on through a never-ending eternity, I ask for no greater glory than to have posterity say, as they tread lightly above my sleeping dust:

"He was worthy to wear a Klansman's robe."

AMEN AND AMEN.

17

Specimen of literary criticism by Prof. Dr. Leonard Doughty, a favorite pedagogue of Texas:

It might have been thought of the Teuton that he

had reached earth's nadir of stupid badness and graceless shame in Hauptmann and Sudermann and their frowzy compeers. But the race that could produce Sudermann and Hauptmann and their like knows no nadir of mental sordidness or moral perversion; there are depths below all other depths for them. The actual, original " scientific " writings of Krafft-Ebing are less vile and pervert than the current " literature " of the Germans today. The stain of that yellow, bastard blood is upon much of the " authorship " of the United States. It is only a matter of procuring a grade-school " education " under our free system and Americanizing an ungainly name. Except for these, the modern " authorship " that makes the " books " upon our stalls is of those dread middle races, Aryan, indeed, but interminably mixed and simmered in the devil's cauldron of middle Europe, and spewed out of Italy and France, and off the dismal Slavic frontiers, and out of that dismal and cankered East, that like a horde of chancre-laden rats are brought to swarm down the gang-planks of a thousand ships upon our shores. It is the spawn of the abysmal fecundity of this seething mass, which now, with the mental and moral deficiency of a thousand generations of defective parentage and low breeding behind and within them, emits these " volumes," as the insane emit shrieks or as a putrid corpse emits odor. After some inquiry I have learned to a confident surety that no one of the " writers " of all this unhappy array was in the service of the United States in the great war.

18

The Jerusalem of patriotism reported to the eminent *Herald* of El Paso by the Hon. Wayne Wright, of Dallas:

One finds possibly the healthiest civic pride in Texas

245

in Abilene. There is a standing offer to anyone who can go to Abilene and feign knocking the town on a street corner and get away with it.

19

Contribution to the Texas Gesta Romanorum by the Rev. W. B. Hogg, an eminent divine of El Paso:

A poor man was shot through and through in Mississippi. His friends rushed to him and said, "Pray." He said, "I did not do it when I was living, and I am too much of a man to do it when I am dying." His old mother came to him and asked him to pray. He said, "Mother, I can't, but if you want to help me, get hold of God." His old mother pulled heaven down around him in prayer, and this man promised God that he would serve Him. He got well, and was admitted into one of the leading churches and lived a good life two years. When he was dying he sent out for all the rounders to come in and watch a man die for God. In his last moments he exclaimed, "Earth is receding; heaven is opening." Better have your trunk packed, your ticket bought, your baggage checked! God's limited may pull in tonight!

20

From a communication to brother Elks by the Hon. Jack Burk, of Lodge No. 216, San Antonio, Texas:

Every setting sun that goes down upon a dying day and leaves the world to darkness and to dreams sheds its last rays upon the kneeling form of thousands who bless the Elks.

21

Example of the pulpit style of the Rev. J. Frank Norris, D.D., a gifted Baptist pastor of Houston:

The silence of the present-day pulpit on the subject of hell is the reason why we are in a hell of a fix now.

22

The Higher Learning at the University of Texas, as described in a public bull by the Hon. L. H. Stark, president of the board of regents:

I am not opposing the selection of men on the university faculty because they have liberal views, but I do and will continue to oppose all those who are not God-fearing men. And we will not have any Socialists up there.

23

Editorial in the *Alcade*, the alumni publication of the University of Texas, on the recent triumph of Fundamentalism in the Board of Regents of that eminent seminary:

We are advised that the Board of Regents of the University of Texas recently passed a resolution requiring the belief in God as a supreme being as a prerequisite to employment in the University, and denying employment to atheists, agnostics, and infidels. It may be that atheists, agnostics, and infidels have a right to be taught by their own kind, but the fact remains that the citizenship of Texas is fully ninety per cent Christian in belief, whether it is in practice or not. This is a country of God-fearing people. The majority of the boys and girls who attend the University of Texas come from good homes where the name of God is held in reverence, and there is no reason why, as far as possible, they should not be taught by men and women who do not deny the existence of God. There are many reasons why the Board of Regents was right in passing the resolution, but the one pointed out is sufficient.

24

Exercise in logic by the accomplished editor of the Cuero *Daily Record*:

An old man 81 years of age was knocked down by a passing car and his condition is serious. Either one of two things is apparent in these frequent knockings down of old people by autoists: either the old folks walk too slow or the car drivers drive too fast.

25

From the opinion of the learned Lattimore, J., in the case of Hatten vs. the State, handed down on June 4 last in the Court of Criminal Appeal of Texas and reported in 263 Southwestern Reporter, 312:

It is true that the parties are Negroes, but they appear to give testimony in every way worthy of belief.

26

Specimen aphorisms by the gifted editorial writer of the Houston *Chronicle*:

No matter how we may respect them in other respects, we cannot admit that our ancestors were right with regard to strong drink. We cannot mention it, or allude to it in such a way as would create the impression that we might think they were right.

Granting the right of free speech, why should it be exercised at times and under circumstances which irritate people?

27

Exultant gloat of the great Christian journal, the eminent *Express* of San Antonio:

More Methodists are reading the daily newspapers today than ever before, and more Methodists are editors, publishers and writers of the newspapers than ever in the history of the church.

28

Gleaned from an Associated Press dispatch from the same town:

Beethoven Hall, headquarters of the San Antonio Ku Klux Klan . . .

29

From an harangue to the Kiwanis Club of San Antonio by Major William G. Morgan, U.S.A.:

The ignorance of the American people as regards their own ignorance is a most remarkable thing.

30

Specimen of elegiac verse from the Cuero *Weekly Record:*

A SAD, SAD EVENT

The Angel of Death has felt no mercy
    Tho He knoweth best.
A tender bud He plucked from our neighbor's garden
    But He wanted another,
A flower just expanding in the holy bonds of ceremony.
    He leaves his life mate,

Who now suffers the torture of living,
But in the beyond, reunion is a blessed comfort.
A mother's heart, who gave and must give again,
   Has been torn to shreds,
Which time, only, can heal.
Life is darkness, then sunshine,
Darkness, than sunshine forever.
From our little village, death has claimed little Linwood
   Dedear,
A child whom God loved better,
The now raging disease, measles with pneumonia,
   taking him home.
   Then, oh! bitter truth!
Another must go, a brother of he who has gone, Adam
   Dedear,
A bridegroom of a few months, succumbed to the
   extraction of one eye, having been abscessed
   beyond cure.

31

Restoration of Christian harmony in the wilds, as reported
by a United Press dispatch from Fort Worth:

The Knights of the Ku Klux Klan here have organized an amateur baseball team and the team has been
admitted to the Fort Worth Amateur Association. In
the same league is a team organized by the Knights of
Columbus. The schedule for the season calls for several
games between the two teams. The practice field is
bounded by a cemetery for Jewish people, and on the
other side is a Catholic hospital. The uniforms of the
players will bear a flaming cross on a white background,
while the letter " K " will adorn the cap.

32

The New Jurisprudence where men are all he, as described by the Hon. Ponder S. Carter, LL.B., city attorney of El Paso:

It took some time for us to find a law under which we could prosecute a man for operating a punch board. We could not use the charge of operating a lottery because the punch board is usually arranged by some other person or company. The charge of gaming could not be used because the operator is not actually placing his ability against that of the player. We found, however, that we could prosecute under a charge of selling lottery tickets because the operator of the punch board technically sells chances or tickets to a lottery arranged by a third person.

33

Rise of civilized feeling in the Gulf littoral, as revealed by a placard in a dime museum at Galveston:

DO NOT SPIT ON
THE BIRDS, MONKEYS
OR SNAKES!

34

Campaign announcement of the Hon. Thomas Lycurgus Walker, candidate for mayor of Houston:

For 18 months something had been tugging at my heart. I could feel it pulling me. I can't explain it to you, but it was tugging, tugging, day and night. I knew what it was.

Then, thirteen months ago, an old Negro came to my shop. He said: " Mr. Walker, the Good Lord is going to call you to a great mission. He wants you for a great service to these people."

I got down on my knees and prayed that night, just as I pray every night of my life. I asked for divine guidance. And the Lord answered me, just as he does all his righteous children who call on him. I was not called to run by the politicians, but by Divine Power.

35

Psychological exhibit from *Col. Mayfield's Weekly*, a Ku Klux journal published at Houston:

Dear Editor: I hope you will forgive me for writing to you. I am a true Protestant of America. I see in your paper that the Ku Klux Klan gives protection for women. I have lived in Marshall for 35 years, and there is not a man in Marshall or anywhere else that can point the finger at me. I have lived an honest life and I just want to know why it is that some people can get protection from the klan and others can not. Now, I have believed in the klan. I think they do a good work. I voted for a man just because I was told he was a klansman. Now there was a Negro named Levie Butts lives just across the street from me. He brought some groceries here. I met him at the door to take the groceries. He says, " I will take them in," or he was coming in. He asked me how I felt. I told him I was not well. I felt bad. I moved back the things that were on the table and then got back from the table. He leaned over on the table and looked at me and says: " Mrs. Morris, you are fat " and grabbed at the front of my dress. I jumped back and said: " You must not talk to me and do that way." Then he eased up and said, " Excuse me." And when I saw he had changed I said no more, for I thought it best to get off if I could, for he is a mean Negro. I saw him go on a white man's place and take his gun from him and jump on him. I would have you to law, but I have never seen any justice in law. They might have fined him and let him out and I wanted him to leave. I don't want to live by that Negro. So I was so sure that the klan would make him leave I didn't ask them to kill him, although he needs it. Mr. Morris wanted to go to him, but I would not let him, for I knew that he would have to go to kill or be killed, and he is not a good shot, and he has no health. He is weak. We did not know the klan, and no one would go with my husband.

Then the Negro went to a white man to get him to help him out, and said that I mistook his meaning. The man would not do it. Then another man, the nearest neighbor that we had, came and said he knew some of the klan and he would see them. Just let it die down and they would get the Negro. So we waited. Every day or two he would come to see what we had done. Mr. Morris told him that he was going to try and see some of the klan. He says, " No, I have done that. You are not to know anything about it. They will do it." So we waited and nothing done. He kept putting us off. This man's wife said she would not ask anyone to go with her. She would do it herself; that the Negro would not have done her that way. How was I to know that the Negro was going to do so, and this man's brother's widow said there was nothing to it. I got afraid and mistook the Negro's meaning.

I call on God, Jesus Christ and heaven that I told the truth, and God knows it nearly kills me to see white people put me down worse than the Negro. I feel like I was going crazy. I can't look out of my door without seeing Negroes. When I saw they were not going to make him leave I told the Negro's wife that the mob was

253

talking of taking him, and the best thing for them to do was to leave. She said, " Oh, they won't do anything to Mr. Butts."

A friend of mine has been giving me your paper to read. I read every word of it. I think just like your paper says. As soon as I can I am going to take your paper and get those Catholic books. I don't like the Catholics, but I do believe in the klan, and I think that Negro paid that man to help him. If you say anything about this, please don't call my name, as it would do no good. Please tell me, was I right or wrong, and forgive me for troubling with this. I could not help writing.

Marshall, Tex., Route 5, Box 7

UTAH

The Higher Learning among the Latter Day Saints, as reported by the Salt Lake *Tribune*:

> Dr. Levi Edgar Young, professor of Western history in the University of Utah, said that in H. G. Wells' " Outline of History " that eminent writer pictures the great epochs of world development, and tells of the coming of Moses, the rise of Greek philosophy, the dawn of intellectual liberty, the French revolution, and finally the modern age of invention. But Dr. Young held that the historian had neglected to set down the most important event in the history of the modern world. That was the organization of the Mormon church in 1830, and the consequent restoration of the true gospel to the world.

2

From a press-sheet issued by the publicist of the National Canners' Association:

> Unique in the history of the National Canners' Association is the fact that its fifteenth president is a poet. Hailing from Utah, and known as the " Poet of the Wasatch Mountains," James A. Anderson, one of the most successful canners of the country, has made quite a name for himself as a writer of verse, as is attested

255

by the following poem, "That Great Big United States."

When you ask what place I love the best—
There is no East, there is no West—
It's just one big, broad land to me,
With a host of friends and opportunities.
North and South both have their charm:
One is cool, the other warm.
Then, why not take the broad view
That God intended all for you?

VIRGINIA

1

Music criticism in the distinguished *Virginian-Pilot* of Norfolk:

> The concert opened with the " Cavalleria Rusticana," of Mascagni, executed with chords expressive of a sighing symphony interspersed with strains caught and held with an intensity of dramatic volume admirably effective. ... After rendering a descriptive symphony by Goldmark the tender strains of Mendelssohn were sounded in a delicate fashion interpretative of moon kissed gardens and the allure of youth and beauty and life and love.

2

Law Enforcement news from the same eminent seaport:

> Just as the jury in the case of Julia Rose, a Negress, charged with selling liquor, was filing out to the jury room in the Federal court, there was a dull thud, and lying in the wake of the jury on the soft carpet was a half-pint of liquor.
>
> S. C. Burgess, a Prohibition agent, won over a half dozen other attaches and officials in a dive for the bottle.
>
> " Where did this come from? " Judge Groner demanded.
>
> Burgess explained he found it on the floor.
>
> " Did one of the jurors drop it? " the court asked.
>
> Nobody knew. Before anything further happened,

the jury reported back with a verdict of guilty and the incident was closed.

3

The latest in fraternal orders in the Old Dominion, as reported by the esteemed Lynchburg *News*:

Joppa Sanctorum, No. 233, of the Oriental Order of Humanity and Perfection, will celebrate its first anniversary Saturday evening. A. Leslie Stephens is the Grand Hyastite.

4

Decay of the spoils system and rise of the technical expert in the Old Dominion, as reported by the Roanoke *Times*:

William F. Drewry, M.D., for 37 years in the service of the State caring for the insane, has accepted an appointment as city manager of Petersburg.

5

State of the enlightenment, as reported by the worthy *Nation*:

Two hundred excited persons, gathered before Magistrate Bell in Princess Anne County, Va., accused 70-year-old Annie Taylor of witchcraft. Whether convinced or not that Annie could kill a mule by waving a cane at him, queer the rising of good corn bread, or put snakes in a woman's stomach, the court banished her to North Carolina.

6

Examples of neo-Confederate English from examination papers submitted by Virginia schoolmarms attending the Summer School at the University of Virginia:

He run down the street, but it was too late to cought him . . .

I like James Witcomb Rily, because he is not dead, and writes poems in the paper that one can see all right . . .

The flames shot into the sky a few foot above the house . . .

7

Law Enforcement news from Norfolk, as reported by the eminent *Virginian-Pilot* on the authority of the Rev. David Hepburn, superintendent of the Virginia Anti-Saloon League:

He said that a large per cent of the juries in Virginia were church members. Yet in some communities, he said, it is extremely difficult for a prosecuting attorney to get a conviction in a liquor case. In this connection he mentioned a recent case in the Henry County Court, which gained considerable publicity at the time of its occurrence. In this case, he said, the defendant admitted his guilt, and yet the jury refused to bring in a verdict for conviction.

" We need more men of the courage demonstrated by Judge T. Turner Clement on that occasion when he ordered the clerk to strike the names of those jurors forever off the jury list," Dr. Hepburn declared. Lethargy in law enforcement, he said, was reflected in the record made in Norfolk last July. Forty-four arrests were made by the police. Of this number, four defendants confessed guilt. Only three of the others were found guilty by juries.

8

Narrow victory of civic evolution in the foothills of the Little Walker mountains, as reported by a dispatch from Pulaski to the celebrated Baltimore *Sunpaper:*

> Cows were banished from Pulaski streets in a referendum election today by a majority of two. There were 417 votes against and 415 for.

9

Beginnings of a horrible doubt in the mind of the gifted editor of the Petersburg *Progress:*

> We confess that for years we regarded alcohol as one of the agents chiefly responsible for crime in the world. Yet, losses by larceny, burglary and embezzlement are over six times as great as they were while we had the saloon and before the Eighteenth Amendment or the Volstead Act was ever heard of.

10

Note on the progress of civilization in Richmond, from the Indianapolis *Fiery Cross:*

> Acca Temple, Ancient Arabic Order Nobles of the Mystic Shrine, are planning a $1,000,000 mosque which is to rank as one of the finest in the nation. It is to have a roof garden which, it is said, will be the largest in the world. The building is to be of Mohammedan architecture and will contain a tile swimming pool,

75 feet by 18 feet; a gymnasium, 126 feet long, large enough for indoor baseball, basket ball and races, and two billiard rooms. There is to be an individual steel locker for every noble and a checking room large enough to accommodate the hat and coat of every member of the temple. The band, patrol, drum corps and chanters will each have private rooms, with separate drill rooms, showers, lockers and lavatories. There will be lounging rooms, card rooms, writing rooms, a big library, parlors, retiring and smoking rooms on each floor and 1902 bedrooms, each with private bath, all outside rooms, for resident and transient nobles.

WASHINGTON

Supernatural doings in hustling Seattle as reported by an eye-witness:

There is a minister of the Gospel here, who, when he preaches, his audience see many signs from God, even greater things than was seen around Jesus. Some see his head become like the sun, some see his face split open, and a center face come out that was so bright that he couldn't look at it, some see the nail prints of the crucifixion in his feet, some see an illuminated cross behind him, and a smaller one on either side. Some see a cross on a post in front of him while he is talking, and when he would lift his hands from the table, it would disappear, and then they get a voice from Heaven saying, " Now do you believe? " Some say they have reasons to believe it is the second coming of the Lord, for they see him in visions, and get presentments of a man with the appearance of this man Sawlt, and they understand it is God; but when they come to Seattle they find it was only Sawlt that they saw. His name is mentioned 40 times in the scripture. Even Jesus prophesied of him, and spoke of it as H-I-S, and said he was God. His followers think so, for they even kiss his hands and feet. I have seen him raise the dead three different times, make the lame to walk, the deaf to hear, and the blind to see.

2

Rise of voluptuousness among the Tacoma Calvinists, as reported by the eminent *News-Tribune:*

> That was a splendid reception accorded the great concert tenor, Leon Rice, at the First Presbyterian Church on Sunday morning and evening, where the auditorium was crowded to capacity, fully 2,000 attending and eagerly absorbing the thrilling tones that poured forth from that splendid vocal organ, tones rising and falling with such ease as might some inexhaustible wind of heaven. Yet it was perfect art that controlled that tone production, especially where, at its fullest strength, it finished with pulsating breaths like visible tone waves. One asked, " Does your voice do that to you, or do you do that to your voice? "

3

Law Enforcement in rural Washington, as reported in a dispatch from Seattle to the Curtis papers:

> About 225 members of the I.W.W. were loaded into six automobile trucks near Concrete, Wash., by Sheriff Conn of Skagit county and taken to the Snohomish county line, unloaded and told to keep going. The sheriff and twenty-two deputies marched upon a bridge over the Baker river leading to a hydroelectric plant, where a strike was on, and seized 150 men.

4

From a proclamation issued to the citizens of Seattle by the Sons of the American Revolution, the American

Legion, the Knights of Columbus and the Jewish Welfare Board jointly:

1

George Washington and others of the Continental Congress were " quarrelsome, pettifogging lawyers and mechanics."

2

Our MOTHERS of Colonial days were " hideous women," clothed " in rags."

3

The Declaration of Independence is still debatable.

4

The purposely empty niche in the Sarotoga Monument " should contain THE STATUE OF BENEDICT ARNOLD."

5

THE COLONISTS WERE A BAD LOT

This is exactly what is being taught to your children in MUZZEY'S HISTORY in use in Seattle Public Schools today.

IT CAN BE STOPPED

5

Qualities esteemed in a public man along the Yakima and Columbia rivers, as revealed by a circular issued by the Hon. E. L. French, candidate for Governor of Washington:

During Mr. French's twelve years in the Legislature he voted for the following bills affecting social conditions:
Local option.
Lazy husband act.
Complete Prohibition.

" Red light " abatement act.
Ratifying United States Prohibition.
Single standard in adultery.
Outlawing race-track gambling.
In the 1920 special session of the Legislature, some of
Mr. French's votes on patriotic legislation were:
Flag salute in schools.
Preventing desecration of flag.
Compelling schools to fly a flag.
Barring aliens who claimed war exemption from
citizenship.
Requiring high school students to give year's study
to American history.
Prohibiting exhibition of flag of associations plotting
against Government.
Prohibiting employment as teachers of aliens or of
those whose certificates are canceled for failure to im-
press principles of patriotism upon pupils.

6

Progress of the New Education in Bellingham, as revealed
by the learned *Herald*:

How to dodge automobiles will be a new course of
instruction at the Parrish Junior High-school here.

7

Sad note in the enterprising Yakima *Republic*:

We are not very enthusiastic about ex-Vice President
Tom Marshall's scheme to repeal all the Prohibition
laws and substitute the Ten Commandments for them.
The Commandments are as good as they ever were but
it is a fact which should not be overlooked that a great
many people in Ellensburg, Seattle, Pasco and else-

where are so ornery that complete enforcement of them seems to be impossible. We don't believe it would help any at all to put them on the statute books.

8

One reason why the Pacific Coast 100% Americans are convinced that the Japs are an inferior people and incapable of true civilization, as reported by the eminent Spokane *Spokesman-Review*:

The youngest senior, a Japanese boy, Welly Shibata, who is not yet 15, is valedictorian of his class at the Lewis and Clark High-school. He is graduating in the classical course.

WEST VIRGINIA

1

Ethical pronouncement of a godly group in the proud town of Huntington:

The Men's Bible Class of the Central Methodist Episcopal church, South, by a unanimous vote, after a full and fair discussion, do hereby heartily approve the action of the Ministerial Association of this city, condemning dancing as contemplated by the Y.W.C.A., a thing and practice that will reach to the highest pinnacle known to man and pluck the brightest jewels in all the land and drag them down to degradation and shame and finally to a devil's hell. Dancing is in opposition to the church of God.

BOB SHANK, *President*
J. B. PORTER, *Teacher*

2

Mellow reflections of the gifted chief editorial writer of the Beckley *Post:*

Why write books? Everybody reads the newspapers. ... And the papers are giving the public what is worth reading and knowing along almost every line imaginable.

3

Giving the Gospels a lift in Wheeling, as reported by the *Register*:

The following questions will be discussed Sunday evening by the Rev. William Elliott Hammond, pastor of the Way Temple:

What was the result of your personal interview with Fatty Arbuckle?

Tell us what Arbuckle said when you asked him the secret of his reducing 80 pounds.

Should girls with big feet be dentists?

Do the things buried with the dead affect the soul?

What do you think of Raymond Hitchcock's pet superstitions?

Will mental concentration on our spirit friends attract them to us?

Does constant grief over the death of a loved one affect the soul of the departed one?

Should the United States prepare for the next war?

4

Growing appreciation of the bozart in West Virginia, as revealed by a banner over the main automobile entrance to Parkersburg:

Parkersburg, W. Va.—Birthplace of Harold Tucker Webster, artist, writer, humorist. Entertains the nation with his "Poker Portraits," "Life's Darkest Moment" and "The Beginning of a Beautiful Friendship." Is married, loves the great outdoors and plays a keen game of poker.

5

Social relaxation in the mining region, as described by
the McDowell *Times*, an eminent public journal of those
parts:

> One night last week there was a very nice birthday
> party given by Mrs. Arthur Allen in honor of the thirty-
> sixth birthday of her mother, Mrs. Mitt Banks. A most
> elaborate outlay of everything imaginable good to eat
> was there at the disposal of everybody and believe me
> the people were there in numbers. Everybody seemed,
> too, to have greatly enjoyed themselves immensely.
> There were games of an innocent nature participated in
> and not one ugly word was heard to be uttered during
> the entire evening.

6

The campaign for Law Enforcement as described by the
Civil Liberties Union:

> After making some remarks about the Klan,
> McMillion charged that lumber corporations control
> some of the civil officers. Chief of Police Cochran
> " thereupon rushed up to McMillion and struck him
> over the head with his revolver." Another official,
> Justice of the Peace J. B. Sutton, attempted to strike
> McMillion with a rock; while Constable James Belcher
> jammed a pistol into his face and dragged him to the
> town jail.

7

Advertisement of a mountain Admirable Crichton in the eminent *Lincoln County Republican* of Hamlin:

Do Your Surveying Now——Write
A. C. HAGER
BOX 15——MIDKIFF, W. VA.
RESIDENCE——TEN MILE RIDGE

COUNTY SURVEYOR AND NOTARY PUBLIC

Does Surveying anywhere at all seasons; writes deeds, takes acknowledgments, and other Notary work in Lincoln County.

Minister:——Marries people anywhere in West Virginia.

Sells Bibles, Testaments, Song Books and Hymnals ——sizes, shapes and grades of each. Let us know the books you want.

Farms——Will Sell, Lease, Rent or Buy

Pigs and Hogs:——Raises, Buys and Sells. Write us for the kind you want.

" Good Will to All Men "

WISCONSIN

1

The spread of the cosmopolitan spirit among the schools, gathered from the *Racquet*, official organ of the La Crosse Normal School:

JEFFERSONIAN SOCIETY

Edgar Lee Master was the subject of the Jeffersonian program. . . . Arthur Herman discussed the life of the writer; a review of " Spoon River Anthology " was given by Joseph Volkoff. Mr. John Boyland showed his skill in swinging clubs. The last number of the program was a parliamentary drill by Mr. Heath.

2

Defiance of the Rev. Crompton Sowerbutts, vicar of St. Michael's, North Fond du Lac:

TO UNFAIR CRITICS ONLY

Certain canting long-faced humbugs who pride themselves on their Christianity are performing back door criticisms on what they please to term my " light-heartedness."

I should be far more serious—in fact I ought to go about (in order to please these people) with the look of an undertaker at his duties which he himself would envy. O! you critics I don't know who you are, you may own half of North Fond du Lac, or you may only own a match box; you may be as large as a house and

271

as powerful as a horse. I am not alarmed. If you have anything to say, don't sneak behind my back. Say what you have straight to my face and I'll give you something to think on. Dismal Jimmies, doleful Donalds and woe begone Killjoys, my subject at 10 A.M. will be " *The Joys of Being a Christian*," I hope to see you.

Remember, cant and artificial conventions cripple Christianity. Christ wants men and women with human hearts, loving and responsive. Our master never had much time for shams. Yet today there are so-called humans walking about to save funeral expenses —in which veins runs asses' milk and water whose God is " respectability " who love to be classed as " toney " and " so refined " in fact they are almost ashamed to remember that Christ was born in a stable and for our wretched sins and selfishness died the death of a criminal.

Your unprejudiced friend,
CROMPTON SOWERBUTTS,
Vicar S. Michael's, N. Fond du Lac

3

Workings of the Holy Spirit at Elton, in the Revival Belt, as reported by the pastor of the local Pentecostal Tabernacle:

Brother Jim Jones, who had asthma for sixteen years, was saved and healed and baptized in the Holy Spirit. Also, a preacher by the name of Steel was healed of blindness in one eye for thirteen years. He was prayed for and healed that moment, and shouted aloud, and the noise was heard afar off.

4

Siniſter notice on the magazine table in the public library at Madison, seat of the University of Wisconsin, the Wisconsin Academy of Sciences, Arts and Letters, and the State Hospital for the Insane:

NOTICE!

Help us to find the person who ſteals each week

The Nation

He sneaks it away and then sneaks it back again.

5

Intelleĉtual aĉtivities among the rural conſtituents of the ghoſt of Senator La Follette, as reported by the Oregon (Wis.) *Observer:*

A very intereſting program was given Monday evening at the High School by the Parent-Teachers' Association. A debate on the subjeĉt, Resolved, That a sewing machine is more beneficial to a family than a cow, was handled by Mrs. Park Ames and Mrs. L. E. Pennewell for the affirmative, and George Rasmussen and Dean Smith for the negative. The decision was unanimous for the sewing machine.

6

The moral equivalent of necking among the Badger Calviniſts, as described in a poſter on the grounds of the

Presbyterian Students' Building at the Summer School of the University of Wisconsin:

SUNRISE BREAKFAST
Up with the Early Birds!
Sunday Morning.
Meet here at:

4.30 A.M. Gray Birds (Dawn)
5.00 „ Red Birds (Rising Sun)
6.00 „ White Birds (Light of Day)

Cost price breakfast served on the lawn at the above hours.

Sign up early!

7

Bulletin posted in the show-window of a favorite shop in Milwaukee:

TO MY WORTHY PATRONS:

My agreement for occupancy of these premises expiring with the present month, prompts me, after a great deal of deliberation, to retire, temporarily, at least, from active business.

In announcing this decision, I want to, first of all, take this opportunity of expressing, to all my friends and patrons, my thorough appreciation of their business and confidence entrusted in me these many years; and can only hope that the services I have always endeavored to render and the quality of the delicatessen furnished, can, in a measure, repay you for the faith warranted in me.

Faithfully yours,
HERMAN LUDWIG

8

The Higher Learning at the University of Wisconsin, as glimpsed in the news columns of the eminent Wisconsin *State Journal*:

Wearing his famous green vest, Prof. Carl Russell Fish was introduced as Wisconsin's outstanding tradition to 250 freshmen attending the annual freshman banquet at the University Y.M.C.A. Wednesday night. Professor Fish and his vest were loudly cheered by the new students.

9

Progress of the Law Enforcement campaign in the La Follette Belt, as described in a dispatch from Milwaukee:

Hurley, Wis., a town of 3,188 persons and sixty-one saloons, is going dry. This was indicated when the City Council yesterday refused licenses to ten saloons, cutting the number to fifty-one, or one for every sixty inhabitants.

WYOMING

I

Progress of science in the foothills of the Table Mountains, as revealed by an advertisement in the Green River *Star:*

I will remove tonsils and adenoids at your own home, eliminating the expense of hospital, which is much better for the patient by not being out in the atmosphere and avoiding the contracting of pneumonia. I have one of the best trained nurses to assist me.

276

ALASKA

I

Dreadful news brought out of the snow wastes by the Right Rev. Peter T. Rowe, Bishop of Alaska:

The church has won its fight, and Alaska today is as good as any other section of the country.

HAWAII

Progress of the tone-art in Honolulu, as reported by the weekly paper of the Honolulu Ad Club, the chief organization of up-and-coming go-getters in the archipelago:

C. W. Stetson, secretary of the Army and Navy " Y " at Pearl Harbor, played " Träumerei " and " The Rosary" on drinking goblets filled with varying depths of water. He says it took three years to collect those goblets. To many in the audience it was a new trick and brought forth a storm of applause. But Stetson had another up his sleeve. He brought forth an old hand-saw and a fiddle-bow, and introduced 98 per cent of the audience to real backwoods music for the first time. More saw-mill harmony was produced with a flock of circular saws which Stetson had trained to tinkle out " Old Black Joe " and " Mother McChree." A good time was had by all.

Results of the Americanization movement in the Pacific, as reported by the Honolulu *Times*:

Mayor John H. Wilson walked from his chair at the board of Supervisors at adjournment this afternoon and hit Supervisor Ben Hollinger in the jaw, breaking his teeth and knocking him against the wall.

From behind, Supervisor Ahia struck the mayor and was floored by Louis Cain and others.

When Ahia got up the mayor turned from Hollinger, who showed no fight, and, wheeling Ahia around by the arm, struck him.

Blood flowed from the mouths of both Hollinger and Ahia as they were escorted from the room.

THE PHILIPPINES

I

Proof that the Filipinos are still barbarians and unfit for self-government, and that the withdrawal of General Leonard Wood and his cossacks would resign them to anarchy:

Manila Monday Musical Club
Twenty-second Season
1923-1924
Sixth Program
Monday, January 14, 1924
5.45 P.M.
Little Theatre Auditorium

Franz Schubert: Octette, Opus 166
   I.   Adagio: Allegro.
  II.   Andante un poco mosso.
 III.   Scherzo: Allegro vivace.
 IV.   Andante con variazione.
  V.   Menuetto: Allegretto.
 VI.   Andante Molto: Allegro.

First Violin—Professor Bonifacio Abdon
Second Violin—Mr. Pedro Antonio
Viola—Mr. José Carrion
Violoncello—Mr. Fillipe Marin
Contrabass—Mr. Joaquin Reyes
Clarinet—Mr. Felix Bascon
French Horn—Mr. Gregorio Fernando
Bassoon—Mr. Antonio Aprecio

PORTO RICO

I

From an interview with Dr. Octavio Jordan, a member of the Porto Rico Senate, in the Philadelphia *Bulletin*:

The first Prohibition enforcement officer sent to Porto Rico came into the Unionist Club in San Juan, where all the government officials and others were passing the evening. He called for a bottle of Scotch and was served immediately. The minute he got his hands on the bottle he stood up and waved it at the crowd and said like an actor, "I have the evidence." The president of the club walked over, took the bottle and said: "I am going to give you something besides the evidence, and you'll be ashamed of it for a long time to come." He laid the agent over the table, took off his dancing slipper and paddled him ten times.

THE VIRGIN ISLANDS

I

Extension of the boons of freedom to St. Thomas, as
reported in a current press dispatch:

Rothschild Francis, editor of the St. Thomas *Emanci-
pator*, has been convicted of political libel and sentenced
to 30 days in jail. He was tried without a jury before a
judge who is his political enemy, and whose appointment he opposed. The libel consisted in charging an
unnamed policeman with brutality.

IN PARTIBUS INFIDELIUM

Letter to the editor of the Paris edition of the New York *Herald* from Miss Flora C. Rhees, a patriotic California lady, z.Z. in Seville:

Perhaps it would be of interest to you and my American friends, especially of Pasadena, Cal., my home, to learn that I am staying at the Hotel de Madrid, Seville, Spain. On the night of February 1, I went to the railroad station, learning that the King, who was here on a visit, was to leave for Madrid.

Taking an interpreter with me, I obtained permission to pass through the gates, where were gathered many officers and military guard. I was right in front of a happy, anticipating crowd. The King arrived and stopped and spoke to various official groups gathered there. Then, when he reached where I was standing, he came forward, shook hands and in exceedingly good English asked me if I was an American and said he hoped to visit America some time, and of course I said he must come to California and our beautiful Pasadena, which, he said, he hoped to do.

(Miss) FLORA C. RHEES.

2

Associated Press cable from Berlin:

Owen D. Young, American member of the expert committee investigating Germany's finances, has had a radio set installed in his hotel apartment so he can listen to concerts when not engaged in discussing financial problems with his fellow experts and their advisers.

Their are four grand opera companies in Berlin, and numerous big symphony orchestras are playing Wagner, Beethoven and the moderns nightly, while a score of companies are singing lighter operas, and myriad concerts are occurring daily and nightly.

With this mass of material to choose from Mr. Young and his American associates take the course of the tired American business man and listen in on radio concerts whenever they have leisure.

3

Why the Marines love the job of civilizing Haiti and Santo Domingo, from the *Star*, published by the Second Brigade at Santo Domingo City:

GARDEN OF EDEN

We announce that we have the choicest selection of wines and liquors in the City of Santiago.
Visit me and visit Heaven on earth!

JOHN'S PLACE

Come and tell your troubles to an ex-Marine who knows good cold beer and good chow. I am located in front of the radio station.

AMERICAN BAR

The Colonel's Place
Come over and sample my choice selection of Beverages. Cold drinks at all times.

4

Extension of the methods of the Anti-Saloon League to the oceans beyond the twelve-mile limit, as revealed by an advertisement in the *Ocean Post*, the daily wireless newspaper of the Holland-America Line:

INTERESTING FACTS ABOUT
SMUGGLING

Under the Tariff Act of 1922 (Section 593), anyone who knowingly and wilfully smuggles jewelry, precious stones, pearls, or any other dutiable merchandise into the United States,

" shall be deemed guilty of a misdemeanor and on conviction thereof shall be fined in any sum not exceeding $5,000, or imprisoned for any term of time not exceeding two years, or both, at the discretion of the court."

The United States Government will pay 25 per cent of any amount up to $200,000, recovered in duties, fines or penalties, for information leading to the detection of smuggling or seizure of dutiable merchandise.

Information relating to jewelry smuggling may be sent, by cable, wireless, or letter, to the

AMERICAN JEWELERS PROTECTIVE ASSOCIATION
Nos. 17-19 West 45th Street
New York City

(Cable or Wireless Address: PROTECTIVE, NEW YORK) or may be given to United States customs officers on the steamer or on the pier.

The name of anyone giving information to the American Jewelers Protective Association *will not be divulged, even to the Government officials.* The Association will colle¢t the award and turn it over to the informant in full.

5

How the uplift is made to pay in Haiti, as described by M. Pierre Hudicort, a Senator of that dark republic:

With the alleged purpose of ſtimulating Haitian agriculture, the American Occupation eſtablished an Agricultural School at Port au Prince. The American dire¢tor of this school receives $15,000 a year. He has imported American " professors" who receive from $500 to $600 a month, but are unable to speak French, and have to have interpreters to translate their remarks to their ſtudents.

NOTES FOR FOREIGN STUDENTS

Alabama—This State is in the heart of the Black Belt and runs chiefly to cotton fields, but of late its coal and iron have made it rich, and so its cities all have country clubs, Rotarians and yellow newspapers. Its principal statesman is the Hon. Oscar W. Underwood, a rich lawyer and Senator. He has been a candidate for the Presidency for years. Inasmuch as all respectable white persons in Alabama are Democrats, the Hon. Mr. Underwood calls himself one, but he is actually a high tariff Republican of the Coolidge model. He now promises to retire from public life. The State is aristocratic in tradition, and has a charming social life. Its capital, Montgomery, was the original capital of the Confederate States.

Arizona—Here we are in a desert, physically and intellectually. Arizona contains no statesmen, nor, indeed, any other inhabitants of a superior kidney. Its towns have such names as Tombstone, Phœnix, Flagstaff, Chloride, Salomé, Painted Rock and Snowflake. The most interesting things in it are the ruins of the ancient Indian villages. The surviving Indians, like the whites, devote themselves chiefly to politics and alcohol.

Arkansas—Arkansas was settled by what the Southern Americans call poor white trash, *i.e.*, whites on the cultural level of the Negroes. It is very religious, and is a stronghold of the Ku Klux Klan. Its chief statesman, the Hon. Joe Robinson, attracted notice some time ago by assaulting a fellow golfer during a game at a Washington golf club. He is the leader of the Democrats in the United States Senate, has ability, and aspires to the Presidency. Arkansas supports a State university at which 1500 boys and girls from the hills and swamps pursue what is regarded in those parts as the higher learning. It has some of the worst clergymen in America. It advocates Prohibition and drinks moonshine.

California—This State, in its early days, was peopled by a hardy and adventurous folk, including many fugitives from justice, and in consequence life there was full of charm. But of late it has been overrun by retired country bankers, cattle-dealers and other such petty rogues from the Middle West, and the old charm has vanished. Los Angeles, its largest city, is run by Christian business men. Any visitor suspected of harboring radical economic views is clubbed by the police and sent to jail. The courts of California are the worst in the United States. Just outside pious Los Angeles is Hollywood, a colony of moving-picture actors. Its morals are those of Port Said.

Colorado—This is a mountain State. Denver, its chief city, is a mile above sea-level. Colorado is now under control of the Ku Klux Klan, and in consequence it has no intellectual life.

Connecticut—Little Connecticut, with but 4800 square miles of area, lies just outside New York City, and is made up, in almost equal parts, of golf links and squalid factory towns. There is a university called Yale at New Haven. The people of Connecticut, in the early days, were very sharp traders—in fact, swindlers. They made nutmegs of wood, and sold them in New York. The nickname, Nutmeg State, clings to this day.

Delaware—This is a small and measly State, owned by a single family, the Du Ponts. They made their money manufacturing explosives. Now they spend it quarreling among themselves. Most of Delaware is but two or three feet above sea level. It has no large city, and no person of any consequence has lived in it for half a century.

District of Columbia—The District consists of the city of Washington and a few suburbs. The government is in the hands of Congress. The inhabitants pay taxes, but cannot vote. The principal citizen is always the President of the United States. The population is made up mainly of government clerks, and is poor and abject. There are more cheap lunch-rooms in Washington than in any other American city. It has an art gallery, supported by the government, and the best library in the Western World, but no concert hall, and no good theatre.

Florida—Florida is the Riviera of the Eastern United States. Along both of its long coasts are strings of Winter resorts, many of them very bawdy. The native Floridans in the interior are all Baptists and Ku Kluxers, and suffer from intestinal parasites. The coast resorts, being close to Cuba and the Bahamas, are all very wet. Good whiskey is even cheaper in Florida than in New York. The principal citizen of the State, until his death, was the Hon. William Jennings Bryan, LL.D., who lived at Miami, where he was employed to promote the sale of villa sites to visitors.

Georgia—This is the home of the Ku Klux Klan. Nevertheless, the State shows signs of an intellectual awakening. It has at least one excellent newspaper, the *Enquirer-Sun*, published by Julian Harris at the little town of Columbus. The sports of the people are such things as lynchings and Methodist revivals. Georgia is one of the wettest of American States. Its hills are full of moonshine distilleries.

Idaho—The only thing heard of Idaho is that it is the home of the Hon. William E. Borah, one of the most influential of United States Senators. So far as is known, no other civilized person lives in it. It lies in the Far West, and is mountainous and desolate.

Illinois—The chief town of Illinois is Chicago, the most thoroughly American of all American cities. The rest of the State consists of farms, and now makes no noise in the world, though Abraham Lincoln came out of it. Chicago has produced some of the best American poets, notably Carl Sandburg and Edgar Lee Masters. But its distinction as a literary center is passing. It has a higher murder rate than any other large city in the world.

Indiana—Indiana used to be notable for the number of authors it produced, especially novelists. But that was thirty years ago. Today it seems to be dead intellectually. The Ku Klux Klan is in control of its politics. It has an almost incredibly drastic State law for the enforcement of Prohibition, but remains very wet. Its towns are all dull and drab.

Iowa—One of the principal Cow States. Its peasants are very rich, and in every farmhouse there is a phonograph, a telephone and a radio outfit. When an Iowa farmer accumulates a competence, he sells out and goes to Los Angeles, in California, to live. The State is very religious, and its principal statesman is one Kenyon, who invented a way to punish immorality by taking from the accused his constitutional right to a jury trial. For this service to God he has been elevated to the Federal Bench. Iowa, of late, has developed a school of very promising writers; they are mainly concerned with the life of its peasants. It has two universities, each with 8000 students.

Kansas—A prairie State, strongly Methodist in theology. In its early days it was much beset by plagues of locusts and grasshoppers, but of late it has grown rich. It has produced many statesmen, all of them strongly in favor of Prohibition. It is one of the wettest States in the

Middle West. One of its chief citizens is E. W. Howe, perhaps the most realistic of American philosophers. His system teaches that wealth is the supreme good. His writings are widely read throughout America, and greatly admired.

Kentucky—A state formerly given over to whisky-drinking, horse-racing and other forms of high living, but now submerged in Methodism. The late Col. Henry Watterson, editor of the Louisville *Courier-Journal* and a celebrated *bon vivant*, was once its most eminent citizen. Now the *Courier-Journal* supports Prohibition. The causes of the collapse of the Kentucky *Kultur* are mysterious, and remain to be explained. The greatest poet Kentucky has yet produced, Madison Cawein, made his living as cashier in a gambling-house. The chief living statesman of the State is the Hon. Augustus Owsley Stanley, an ardent wet. The Prohibitionists lately retired him to private life. Nevertheless, very fair whiskey is still to be had in Kentucky.

Louisiana—A Southern State, mainly swamp. The delta of the Mississippi river divides it into two parts. Its chief city, New Orleans, was settled by Frenchmen and Spaniards, and was until lately the scene of a charming social life. It had, for many years, the only opera house in the South, and the only good restaurants. Recently it has been invaded and ruined by 100% Americans. Rural Louisiana is mainly Methodist, and runs to barbarous lynchings. The climate is very hot. There are no inhabitants of any importance.

Maine—Maine went dry long before the national Prohibition Act was adopted. As a result, its people early attained to proficiency in the trade in contraband liquors. They are now largely occupied by bootlegging from Canada, which adjoins it to the North. Though it is in the East, it is still a wild State, with extensive forests. Along the Atlantic coast are many Summer resorts, all of them wet. Maine is as dead, intellectually, as Abyssinia. Nothing is ever heard from it.

Maryland—Called the Free State because its mores prohibit jailing men for their opinions. Even during the World War, no one was so jailed there. Maryland is very wet, and the State Legislature has refused to pass an act for the enforcement of Prohibition. Its principal statesman is the Hon. A. C. Ritchie, LL.D., now its governor, and famous as the handsomest politician in America. He is, like all other Marylanders of condition, wet. The State is known for its attractive social life, and has the best cooks in the United States, most of them Negroes. Its one big city, Baltimore, has half the population of the whole State.

Massachusetts—The principal State of New England, and for long the chief stronghold of the Puritans. Now they have fallen into decay, and Massachusetts is run by the children of more recent immigrants, mainly Irishmen. Harvard University, at Cambridge, is the most fashionable American university. President Coolidge was formerly governor of Massachusetts. The principal city, Boston, is very wet. Since the death of the Hon. Henry Cabot Lodge, LL.D., the State has no statesman.

Michigan—Michigan is the seat of Henry Ford, the billionaire automobile manufacturer. Its chief city, Detroit, is mainly devoted to making automobiles, and is immensely rich. Canada is separated from Detroit by a narrow river; thus the city is tremendously wet. The rest of Michigan is negligible—farms and forests, inhabited by a half-civilized peasantry. At Ann Arbor there is a State university with 10,000 students. In 1924 the British Poet Laureate lived there for a few months, and was politely gaped at. The Detroit intelligentsia begin to show a considerable literary activity.

Minnesota—A Cow State, mainly settled by Swedes. It inclines toward radicalism in politics, especially when the crops are poor. It has two cities, St. Paul and Minneapolis. They are but a few miles apart, and hate each other terrifically. It is dangerous to his life and limb for a St. Paul bootlegger to visit Minneapolis, or vice versa. The State has no statesmen, poets or painters, but there is a good symphony orchestra at St. Paul. It is celebrated as the birthplace of Sinclair Lewis, author of " Main Street " and " Babbitt," both of which describe its life.

Mississippi—This State is in the heart of the Black Belt, and has more Negro inhabitants than whites. It is controlled by the Methodists and Baptists and is very dry, but its principal statesman, the Hon. John Sharp Williams, now retired, is wet. There are few cities, and all are small; thus there is little intellectual life. The State has some of the worst newspapers in America.

Missouri—The principal city of Missouri is St. Louis, which, before Prohibition, had the largest breweries in the United States. The State is still very wet. It was settled largely by Germans, with a sprinkling of Frenchmen from down the Mississippi River. The chief statesman is the Hon. James A. Reed, a dominating personality in the United States Senate and a vigorous defender of the historic liberties of the American people. Its other politicians are all ninth-rate.

Montana—This State is in the Rocky Mountains, and is largely uninhabitable. Its chief statesman is the Hon. Thomas J. Walsh, an able but somewhat romantic man, barred from the Presidency because he is a Catholic. Another figure in its life is the Hon. Burton K. Wheeler, whose exposures of thievery at Washington so alarmed the Coolidge administration that efforts were made to jail him on false charges of personal corruption. Aside from Walsh and Wheeler there is no one in Montana of any consequence. The chief industry is copper mining.

Nebraska—A typical Cow State. The inhabitants, with few exceptions, read the Bible daily. When they accumulate enough money, they sell out their farms and go to Los Angeles. The State university at Lincoln is superior to most other universities in the Middle West. There are no large cities.

Nevada—This is a mining State, mainly desert. It has very liberal divorce laws, and in consequence is visited by swarms of unhappy husbands and wives. In six months they acquire citizenship, and are liberated from their bonds. At Reno, the principal town, there is a large colony of such seekers. Nevada has no intellectual life. The members of the divorce colony occupy themselves by playing golf, watching the calendar, and practising adultery.

New Hampshire—One of the New England States, almost wholly mountainous. It has escaped the degeneration of Massachusetts, Maine and Vermont, and still shows a considerable intellectual vigor. It is known as the Granite State. It has no statesmen. It lies along the Canadian border, and is very wet. In Summer it attracts many holiday-makers.

New Jersey—New Jersey is the wettest of American States. It lies just outside New York City, and its towns are largely peopled by New Yorkers who go into the city every day. But it also has some large towns of its own, notably Newark. On the coast is Atlantic City, the Brighton of America, with dozens of large hotels, and a merry, voluptuous life. Rum ships from the Bahamas ply direct to Atlantic City. The late Woodrow Wilson was once governor of New Jersey. Its chief statesman today is the Hon. Walter E. Edge, who began life as a printer's devil. At Princeton there is a university.

New Mexico—This State is mainly desert. It has a high altitude and is much frequented by invalids. Many Spanish-speaking Mexicans survive in the population. Of late a colony of writers and artists has been set up in the old Spanish town of Taos, and New Mexico has produced a competent novelist, Harvey Fergusson, on its own account. The principal statesman is the Hon. Albert B. Fall, who was Secretary of the Interior in the Cabinet of the late President Harding. Fall is now awaiting trial on a charge of accepting a bribe of $100,000 while in office. The motto of New Mexico is *Crescit Eundo*. It is a dry State meteorologically, but otherwise wet.

New York—New York is the Empire State, with a population of 11,000,000—more than all of New England has, with a half a dozen Western States thrown in. Above half of this population is in New York City. Rural New York is religious and very dry; New York City is anti-nomian and wet. The city pays little heed to the laws of the United States, or to the national mores. It is immensely rich, and devoted to pleasure. There are more harlots in New York than in the whole of Spain. Many of its bootleggers are millionaires. The principal statesman is the Hon. Al Smith, who began life as a fishmonger. He is barred from the Presidency by the fact that he is a Catholic. In the Middle West New York is looked upon as the capital of Satan, and no woman who has ever been there is regarded as a strictly A1 virgin.

North Carolina—This is one of the Southern States, but is far more civilized than the others. It has several good newspapers and a State university at Chapel Hill with a number of able professors. The State begins in swamps on the Atlantic seaboard and ends in high mountains in the West. Its peasants are of a low grade, and mainly Baptists or Methodists. North Carolina is full of moonshiners. Its principal statesman is the Hon. Josephus Daniels, Litt.D., who was Secretary of the Navy in the Cabinet of Dr. Wilson. He is a professing Christian and wears the traditional uniform of a Southern politician, with a boiled shirt, a soft black hat and a black string tie.

North Dakota—This is a remote and God-forsaken Cow State, largely peopled by Scandinavians. Vilhjalmur Stefansson, the arctic explorer, who was born just across the Canadian border, says that North Dakota is colder in Winter than the North Pole. At the first fall of snow the inhabitants barricade their houses, and resort to sleep and prayer. Its capital is called Bismarck.

Ohio—Ohio has supplied more Presidents than any other American State. Its last gift to the nation was the late Dr. Harding, who was poisoned by the Jesuits for opposing their plot to seize control of the government at Washington. Ohio is controlled, politically, by the Anti-Saloon League, and its politics are inordinately corrupt. The inhabitants are mainly Methodists. The principal city, Cleveland, was the seat of John D. Rockefeller before he moved to New York. There is no intellectual life in the State; all of its energies are absorbed by money-getting, religion and bootlegging.

Oklahoma—This State is chiefly given over to oil-drilling. It was settled largely by persons who left the East for the East's good, and remains turbulent and barbarous to this day. Its politicians are almost unanimously thieves. Its towns bear such Indian names as Okmulgee, Pawhuska, Tahlequah and Comanche. In Oklahoma the American frontier is gasping out its last breath. Of late the State has produced a number of young writers of great promise. Its principal statesman, the Hon. Robert L. Owen, is half Indian, and a man of ability.

Oregon—This State is controlled by the Freemasons, who lately forced the adoption of a State law prohibiting private schools, and requiring every child to be educated at the public expense. The aim of the law was to put down the Catholic parochial schools. It was declared unconstitutional by the Supreme Court of the United States. Oregon is seldom heard of. Its people believe in the Bible, and hold that all radicals should be lynched. It has no poets and no statesmen.

Pennsylvania — Pennsylvania is the second largest American State. It was originally settled by Quakers and Germans, and many of the latter, until very recently, scarcely spoke English. Pittsburgh is the center of the American steel industry and has produced scores of millionaires. The State has a corps of Cossacks devoted to putting down strikes by force, and has been the scene of many massacres of workingmen, mainly foreigners. At Philadelphia the enforcement of Prohibition is in the hands of a brigadier general of marines; the city remains one of the wettest in America. Philadelphia is otherwise a dull town, devoted to money.

Rhode Island—This is the smallest of American States. Its land area is but little more than 1000 square miles. It is organized, politically, on the rotten borough system, and of late the inhabitants have been trying to free themselves by armed rebellion. Rhode Island next to New Jersey, is the wettest American State. It is crowded with filthy factory towns, and has no statesmen.

South Carolina—In South Carolina divorce is forbidden by law. This eccentricity gives the State its sole distinction. At Charleston, on the coast, there is a Poetry Society;

the rest of South Carolina is a blank. It has not produced a man of mark since the Civil War.

South Dakota—Nothing much is known about this State, which lies upon a prairie and is peopled almost solely by peasants. Persons who have visited it report that its people are all professing Christians.

Tennessee—In Tennessee a school-teacher was lately fined $100 for teaching Evolution to his pupils. Such heresies are prohibited by a State law. Tennessee is controlled by the Primitive Baptists, and is only half civilized. It has no statesmen. A few poets lurk in one of its so-called universities, but the *Polizei* are preparing to rout them out. It is universally believed in Tennessee that if one puts a horse hair into a bottle of water it will turn into a snake.

Texas—Texas is the largest American State. It is so large that a fast express train consumes more than 24 hours in crossing it. It was very wild in the early days, and is still inhabited largely by he-men with hairy chests. At one time it was an independent republic; it joined the United States in 1845. It has its own flag to this day. The prevailing faith in Texas is the Baptist, and the chief clergy of that persuasion are very influential. But of late there has been a rising of atheism in the towns, and recent travelers report that the more advanced female inhabitants now smoke cigarettes and otherwise flout God. But it is still considered immoral in Texas to wear spats or to dress for dinner. A dry State—and very wet.

Utah—Utah was founded in the desert by the Mormons, and they still control it. Its principal statesman, the Hon. Reed Smoot, is one of the Twelve Apostles of the Church, and has magical gifts. One man stands ahead of him; when that man dies the Hon. Mr. Smoot will succeed to all the awful powers of the late Brigham Young. The Mormons renounced polygamy 40 years ago, but the older ones still cherish their surviving wives. Utah is very rich, but not active intellectually.

Vermont—This is the native State of the Hon. Mr. Coolidge. Otherwise it is a vacuum. It consists mainly of hills.

Virginia—Virginia was once the premier American State, and hatched a long line of statesmen, headed by Washington and Jefferson. It is now controlled, politically, by its poor white trash, and so it produces no more statesmen. Its principal living inhabitant is James Branch Cabell, the novelist. Its university at Charlottesville is dull and reactionary. The people of Virginia, white and black, are mainly believers in baptism by total immersion. Richmond, the capitol, is the only State capitol in America that lacks a public library. Nevertheless, the social life of its surviving gentry is very agreeable.

Washington—This State is on the Pacific Coast, and is still rather primitive. It has no citizens of any importance, and is seldom heard from.

West Virginia—West Virginia is given over to coal mining, and the mine owners control it. When the miners go on strike they are murdered by the State police. Sometimes their women and children are butchered with them. In the remoter mountains of the State the blood feud still prevails, and assassinations are common. The people are all evangelical Christians, and devote their leisure to moonshining. The general state of civilization in West Virginia is that of Albania, Haiti and Afghanistan.

Wisconsin—This State was peopled mainly by Germans, and its principal city, Milwaukee, is almost as German as Munich. Good beer is still on public sale there, despite

Prohibition. The peasants of the State incline to radicalism in politics, and their idol is the late Robert M. La Follette, who was a candidate for the Presidency against Dr. Coolidge in 1924. Wisconsin has a State university with more than 8,000 students. There are professors of swine husbandry and cheese-making. Milwaukee is the only large American city ever to be captured politically by the Socialists.

Wyoming—This is a mountain State, given over to mining and sheep-raising. Its principal statesman is the Hon. Francis E. Warren, who has been called the greatest shepherd since Abraham.

GLOSSARY

Ad Club—An organization of advertising agents.

American Legion—A national organization of veterans of the World War. It consists mainly of conscripts who saw no active service.

Anti-Saloon League—The national organization of Prohibitionists. Its headquarters are in Ohio. In each State it has a staff of propagandists, usually headed by a Methodist clergyman. At Washington it maintains a formidable legal bureau, and exerts heavy pressure upon Congress.

Babbitt—One resembling the hero of Sinclair Lewis' novel of the same name. A generic term used to designate any Philistine.

Bible Belt—That portion of the United States in which the people believe in the literal accuracy of Genesis. It includes the whole country, save only for areas of ten mile radius around the cities of above 100,000 population.

Bible Class—A class of adults, met in a Sunday-school to hear Holy Writ expounded.

Bible Marathon—A form of sport very popular among rural Christians. The Bible is read aloud, in relays. Time is kept, and the congregation which finishes soonest is much applauded.

Black Belt—That portion of the Southern United States wherein the Negroes outnumber the whites.

Blind Pig—An unlawful and surreptitious liquor shop.

Blue—A general synonym for Puritanical. A blue Sunday is one on which the blind pigs and speak-easies are closed.

Blue Grass—The region in which blue grass (*Poa*

301

pratensis) grows. It lies mainly in Kentucky, which is called the Blue Grass State.

Boll Weevil—A snout beetle (*Anthonomus grandis*) that is very deſtructive to growing cotton. It has caused immense damage in the South. The peasants diſtruſt the inseƈticides recommended by the Department of Agriculture, and combat the inseƈt mainly by prayer and sorcery.

Bonus Belt—That part of the United States in which the American Legion is influential in politics. The chief purpose of the Legion is to obtain grants from the public funds for its members.

Booſter—One who devotes himself to advertising his town, usually by gaudy methods.

Bootician—A superior bootlegger. One who sells his goods only by the case, and to the wealthy.

Bootlegger—A dealer in contraband alcoholic beverages.

Bozart—The American spelling of beaux arts.

Buck—A dollar.

Campus—The common yard of a college. It is usually large, and is the scene of many college aƈtivities, including fights.

Chautauqua—A form of rural entertainment. A committee is formed, a huge tent is ereƈted, and in it, for a week or so, various leƈturers, musicians, etc., entertain the peasantry. The chautauqua is the chief arena of American "idealism." It is much frequented by politicians, theologians and professional patriots.

Chirotonsor—A name adopted by the more elegant kind of barbers.

Coca Cola—A popular soft drink, made at Atlanta, Georgia, and drunk by almoſt everyone in the South. It is a sort of birch beer. The proprietor, one Candler, is an eminent Methodiſt, and the brother of a bishop.

Co-ed—A girl ſtudent in a college which admits both

sexes. All of the State universities, save a few in the South, do so. Most co-eds are far more interested in getting husbands than in acquiring learning.

Corn Belt—That portion of the United States in which Indian corn, or maize, is the principal crop. It includes most of the Middle West and a part of the South.

Cow State—A State in which the peasants are mainly herdsmen. Constant association with animals makes them very religious.

Cracker—A native of Georgia, especially a poor farmer from the hills.

Daughters of the Revolution—An organization of women with ancestors who served in the American Revolution. Membership in it confers a certain social distinction, especially in the smaller towns.

Dime—A silver coin worth ten cents.

Dry—One in favor of Prohibition. Most bootleggers are ardent drys.

Eighteenth Amendment—The Prohibition amendment to the national Constitution.

Elk—A member of a popular fraternal order, the Benevolent and Protective Order of Elks. It has club-houses in most towns. The members have sporting tastes, and are generally opposed to Prohibition.

Eminent—Applied to a politician, the word means that he is not actually in jail for corruption. Applied to a newspaper, it means nothing.

Flag Pledge—An oath to defend the national ensign against foreign and domestic foes. In most States it is exacted of school children.

Flivver—A popular name for a Ford automobile.

Foreign Missions Belt—That region in which the peasants contribute liberally to foreign missions. It is co-extensive with the rural sections of the country.

Fourteenth Amendment—This amendment, with the

Fifteenth, was adopted after the Civil War to enfranchise the liberated slaves. It is violated in every Southern State.

Freshman—A college student in his first year.

Fundamentalist—A Christian who believes in the literal authenticity of the Bible.

Go-Getter—A business man of extraordinary enterprise, especially a pugnacious salesman.

Hard Liquor—Any distilled alcoholic beverage.

He-man—One of an obvious and excessive masculinity. Especially, one who drinks his whiskey straight, *i.e.*, without water.

Het up—Excited.

Hobo—A tramp.

Hog and Hominy Belt—That region in which the principal victuals of the peasants are pork and boiled maize. It includes most of the South.

Home-Brew—Beer or ale made at home. It is estimated that 500,000,000 gallons are now made annually in the United States. Brewing has been restored as a domestic art.

Hookworm Belt—That region in which most of the peasants are infested by the hookworm (*Necator americanus*). They become lazy and shiftless, and commonly devote themselves to religion. The Hookworm Belt covers most of the South.

Hoosier—A native of Indiana.

Improved Order of Red Men—A fraternal order whose members array themselves like Red Indians. It flourishes mainly in the small towns.

Infant Damnation Belt—That portion of the United States in which the prevailing religion is the Presbyterian. It lies mainly along the line of the Appalachian Mountains.

Inspirational—Provocative of emotion. An inspirational speaker is one who can make his audience sweat and glow.

Invisible Empire—The mystic domain of the Ku Klux

Klan. When a peasant is initiated into the Klan he becomes a citizen of the Invisible Empire.

Jitney—A term of disparagement. It may be applied to anything or any person, from a Ford automobile to a United States Senator.

Job-Holder—One who occupies public office. A bureaucrat.

Junior—A third-year man at college.

Kiwanis—An organization of luncheon clubs. The members are mainly Babbitts, and lunch in common once a week. There is always a speaker, and the meeting ends with choral singing. Kiwanis is very patriotic. There is a club in almost every American town.

Klavern—The meeting-place of Ku Klux Klansmen. It is usually a hall above a livery-stable.

Kleagle—One of the principal officers in the Ku Klux Klan. He gets a share of every dollar collected from the imbeciles who join the organization.

Knights of Pythias—A national fraternal order. Most of the members are farmers or workingmen.

Lions—A group of luncheon clubs, founded in imitation of Rotary and Kiwanis, but composed, in the main, of men of less opulence.

Live Wire—Any man of energetic disposition, but especially a very active business man.

Lizzie—A popular name for a Ford automobile. Sometimes it becomes Tin Lizzie.

LL.D.—A degree conferred by American universities upon politicians, millionaires, and other men likely to be useful. Among the most eminent American LL.D.'s are Calvin Coolidge and Otto H. Kahn.

Lobbyist—One who devotes himself to influencing legislation, often by the bribery of legislators.

Mail Order Belt—That portion of the United States in which the local shops carry such poor stocks that the people buy most of their supplies from large companies in the big cities, which deliver them by post. It includes most of the South and Middle West.

Mail Order Catalogue—The price list of a mail order company. Many such catalogues weigh three or four pounds. There is one in every American farm-house. The Bible, the almanac and the mail order catalogue constitute the main reading of 50% of the American people.

Main Street—A generic name for the regions lying remote from the large cities. It derives from the title of Sinclair Lewis' novel, and is now very widely used.

Moonshine—Contraband whiskey, usually made by farmers. It is the common drink in the regions where Prohibition is " enforced "—that is, where good liquors are unobtainable. It is drunk fresh from the still, sometimes still warm.

Moonshiner—A maker of moonshine whiskey.

Moose—A member of the Loyal Order of Moose, a fraternal organization, much like the Elks. A Moose is commonly a poorer man than an Elk.

Mortician—An undertaker.

Movie—The common American name for the cinema.

Necking—A form of petting. A girl who has been well necked is never the same again.

New Thought—A system of mystical philosophy, very popular among the uneducated. Its chief tenet is that matter has no existence—that mind is all powerful. Its practitioners profess not only to cure all diseases, but also to reunite separated lovers, to bring worldly prosperity, etc.

New Thoughter—One who believes in the New Thought.

Nickel—A coin worth five cents.

Nineteenth Amendment—The amendment to the national Constitution providing for woman suffrage.

Odd Fellows—A fraternal order with 2,000,000 members.

Old Dominion—A nickname for Virginia.

Open Spaces—The prairies of the West. The absence of cities is supposed to conserve the virtue and Christian orthodoxy of the inhabitants.

Pastorium—Among the Baptists of the South, the home of the pastor. It is provided at the expense of his flock.

Peruna—A popular proprietary medicine. The name is applied figuratively to any sure-cure, even in politics.

Petting—Making love; spooning. Petting may include any carnality short of fornication. It is very popular in the co-educational colleges.

Petting Party—A mixed gathering at which petting and necking are the chief diversions. It is usual, also, to have dancing.

Pounding—A pound party. When a rural pastor runs short of provisions, the members of his flock visit him, each bearing a sack of potatoes, a pound of sugar, a ham, or something else of the sort.

Professor—A title given in rural America to all male pedagogues, even in the elementary schools.

Publicist—A press agent. Every politician, movie actress and prize fighter in America has a publicist. The most eminent member of the order is Ivy Lee, publicist to John D. Rockefeller. Ivy, despite his given name, is a man, not a woman.

Realtor—An estate agent, especially one who opens new suburbs and builds large numbers of houses.

Red—Any man who advocates or believes in any political idea not commonly accepted. In America Nietzsche and John Stuart Mill would be Reds.

Red-blooded—Full of pugnacity, and eager to protect female virtue and the honor of the flag. The American Legion is composed mainly of red-blooded men. So are all lynching parties.

Red-Eye—A name for any raw and raucous whiskey.

Rotarian—A member of Rotary.

Rotary—An organization of luncheon clubs, mainly devoted to hearing " inspirational " speakers.

Rum Row—The line of liquor-laden ships lying 12 miles outside New York harbor.

Sauerkraut—A German dish, extensively consumed in the United States. It is made by fermenting sliced cabbage. During the World War, the government ordered that its name be changed to liberty cabbage, but the old name is now in use again.

Scofflaw—One who scoffs at the Prohibition Act.

Senior—A fourth-year man at college.

Sheba—A voluptuous young woman; one who attracts masculine attention, and likes it.

Sheik—A lady-killer. The word is pronounced *sheek*, not *shike*.

Soft Drink—A drink containing no alcohol.

Sons of the Revolution—A national organization of the descendants of patriots who served in the American Revolution.

Sophomore—A second-year man at college.

Speakeasy—A surreptitious liquor shop.

Stand-patter—One who is very orthodox politically; in particular, one who favors wealth.

Straw Boss—In a factory, the lowest grade of foreman.

Tar-Heel—A native of North Carolina.

Total Immersion Belt—That portion of the United States in which the Baptists are in a majority. It lies mainly in the low, malarious parts of the South.

United Daughters of the Confederacy—An organization of the female descendants of men who served in the Civil War on the Southern side. It is very influential in the South.

University—In America the term is used to designate almost any college, however small. The Oklahoma Baptist University, for example, has but 15 teachers. The

GLOSSARY

Sioux Falls University, at Sioux Falls, South Dakota, has but 100 students.

Up-and-Coming—Full of business enterprise.

Vice Crusade—An effort to put down prostitution. It usually takes on the form of a public orgy, led by the Methodist parsons of the town afflicted. The parsons greatly enjoy the contact with the loose girls.

Volstead Act—The national law for the enforcement of Prohibition, so-called because it was brought into the House of Representatives by the Hon. Andrew J. Volstead, of Minnesota.

Wet—Dripping with alcohol, as, a wet town, a wet congressman, a wet university president. There is also such a thing, in politics, as a wet dry, *e.g.*, a politician who prepares for making a speech in favor of Prohibition by taking three or four stiff drinks. The late President Harding was a wet dry.

White mule—Another name for moonshine whiskey.

Wop—An Italian.

Y.—An abbreviation for Y.M.C.A., *i.e.*, Young Men's Christian Association.

CHISWICK PRESS: CHARLES WHITTINGHAM AND GRIGGS (PRINTERS), LTD.
TOOKS COURT, CHANCERY LANE, LONDON.

MARTIN HOPKINSON AND CO. LTD.

DAI NIHON. By THE REV. GRAHAM MARTYR, Author of
"An Imperial Conspiracy," "Etajima Tales," etc., sometime Instructor at the Imperial Naval College of Japan, Organizing Secretary for the Corean Mission. Printed on deckle-edged paper, with devices by the Author in red. Demy 8vo. Paper boards, canvas back, with headband and silk marker and gilt top. 10s. 6d. net.

THE SACRED GIRAFFE. Being the second volume of the
posthumous works of JULIO ARCEVAL, edited by SALVADOR DE MADARIAGA. Demy 8vo. Cloth. 10s. 6d. net.

A book of fancy and imagination, it creates a world of its own, with its science and its arts, its press and its politics, its love-affairs and its marriage ceremonies and its religion.

THE WORLD OF THE THEATRE. By J. T.
GREIN, WITH A PREFACE BY GILBERT K. CHESTERTON. Demy 8vo. Cloth. 15s. net.

". . . Mr. Grein excels them all in the range of comparisons at his disposal. His experience is vast, his judgment shrewd and independent, and his views are expressed with vivacity and brevity."—*New Statesman*.

MOSUL AND ITS MINORITIES. By HARRY
CHARLES LUKE, Author of "The Fringe of the East," etc., Assistant Governor of Jerusalem, 1920-1924. Illustrated with 26 reproductions of Photographs. Demy 8vo. Cloth. 10s. 6d. net.

"Is a mine of interesting information. . . . It is full of strange lore gathered . . . by one who has sufficient linguistic knowledge to enable him for the most part to dispense with interpreters, and the necessary scholarship to appreciate the true value and meaning of the legends and traditions, as well as the history which he has investigated."—*The Times*.

IN MEXICAN WATERS. By GEORGE HUGH BAN-
NING. Profusely illustrated with photographs reproduced in collotype and half-tone. Medium 8vo. Cloth. 18s. net.

"There is a fine air of adventure about this book . . . he is able to invest the expedition with all the glamour of an Elizabethan merchant venturer."—*Daily Chronicle*.

1700 MILES IN OPEN BOATS. THE STORY
OF THE LOSS OF THE S.S. TREVESSA, IN THE INDIAN OCEAN, AND THE VOYAGE OF HER BOATS TO SAFETY. By CECIL FOSTER, MASTER MARINER, Captain of the S.S. "Trevessa." With many illustrations and three charts. Demy 8vo. Cloth. 10s. 6d. net.

"If the master's book had been written for no other reason than to call our attention to Michael Scully, then that would have been sufficient. . . . But this book by the master of a tramp steamer is a model for young novelists who are impelled to tell the world what life is."
Weekly Westminster.

ISLANDS, WEST INDIAN — ÆGEAN. By SIR
ARTHUR E. SHIPLEY, G.B.E., F.R.S., Master of Christ's College, Cambridge. With many illustrations. Crown 8vo. Cloth. 6s. net.

"The breezily written book will attract and delight the traveller, scientist and business man . . . this eminent professor knows how to impart knowledge without being stodgy."
Journal of Commerce.